STEVIE NICKS

BIOGRAPHY

Life and music about the gold dust lady of Fleetwood Mac

TABLE OF CONTENTS

CHAPTER 1

DAUGHTER OF THE DESERT

CHAPTER 2

FIRST BAND

CHAPTER 3

COCAINE

CHAPTER 4

FLEETWOOD MAC

CHAPTER 5

BELLA DONNA

CHAPTER 6

SARA

CHAPTER 7

24 KARAT GOLD

CHAPTER 1
DAUGHTER OF THE DESERT

Stevie Nicks may have lived a nomadic lifestyle, but Phoenix's subtropical desert temperature and stunning mountain ranges drew her back time and again. Phoenix represented Stevie's roots, and having a sense of home and family is crucial in the erratic life of a rock'n'roll star; Stevie still has a home in Phoenix to this day. The name of the location would serve as a perfect metaphor for Nicks as time passed, that of a gorgeous bird that burned out only to revive from its own ashes, more dazzling than ever. An appropriate symbol for a rock star. Stevie was born under the sign of Gemini, which is associated with the element of air and the planet Mercury. Astrologers may agree that her interest with the skies, mists, and veils, desire for diaphanous stage clothes, and lifelong love of ballet and the notion of the body in flight can all be attributed to cosmic links. After all, her most famous song, 'Rhiannon,' is about a white witch who is 'taken by the sky,' and what are dreams and visions but ethereal glances into the unconscious?

Stevie had always been musically inclined, thanks to her grandfather AJ, a free-spirited musician who lived in the highlands. AJ worked as a pool player, but his main interest was country and western music, and he was an excellent multi-instrumentalist, playing harmonica, guitar, and violin. His desire to be a successful musician prompted him to leave his family and travel across the country, travelling freight trains and performing in bars. Little Stevie was inspired by her bohemian grandfather, and the day he arrived with a trunk full of 45s marked the beginning of her journey and the discovery of her own voice. They sat back-to-back on her bedroom floor, listening to records. "Sing like you mean it, granddaughter," AJ would advise the blonde-haired toddler next to him; "put your heart into it." They quickly became inseparable, and AJ would take four-year-old Stevie to taverns all across the Midwest, where she would sing along with her grandfather and dazzle everyone, already a box-office success. This was her first taste of success, of how she could captivate an audience while earning a few bucks: AJ would pay her 50 cents for her efforts. The Nicks family relocated to Los Angeles when Stevie was very young, opening a Mexican-style bar where her mother would cook and the family's men would hang out, but music flourished even after Stevie began school, and she was becoming increasingly confident, her talent radiating from her, very much in her element while singing in front of an audience. One of Stevie's favourite childhood memories was returning home from school and going by the bar to see her father, uncles, and loving grandfather listening to music and singing together. "I can remember being there at about two in the afternoon," she said to me. "There is no one in there..."I recall singing with my grandfather and realising, even at an early age, that music would be a significant part of my life."

AJ agreed with me. He realised he had a celebrity on his hands and decided to give his granddaughter a tour of sorts. Jess and Barbara wanted to help Stevie, but they weren't sure if sending a five-year-old on tour to play in bars was the best option. It was time to make a decision. Stevie's younger brother Christopher had just been born, and another move, this time to Albuquerque, New Mexico, was on the way - surely enough misery in their lives without their baby daughter fleeing to serve as a miniature Vaudevillian for inebriated strangers? The reaction was a clear 'no,' which AJ refused to accept. Following a fierce argument, he stormed out on the family, refusing to speak with them for the next two years. Stevie's heart was broken by his unexpected absence and terrible blood after being so close to AJ; it was the first of many emotional storms to come. However, the arrival of Chris Nicks was likely a storm in and of itself. Stevie, the self-proclaimed 'little diva,' was 'out of control,' and her parents hoped that having another child would bring some balance to the family and teach Stevie that she wasn't the only one in the world. It did not go well, and it would be years before the siblings got along. "I hated Chris," she admits. "I would pull his hair and kick him...For the rest of my life, I will apologise to him." Her parents were generally harsher with their first child than with their second, but as their only daughter, she was still "the star in my family's sky," as she once dreamily stated, and they nurtured her creativity and love of stories, fairy tales, music, and dancing. Stevie grabbed shawls and swirled them around her room, pretending to be Isadora Duncan, a ballet dancer whose free movement and expressive, exuberant style influenced Stevie's own way of moving. Going to a strict ballet

Praise for Aurora Rey

Lambda Literary Award Finalist
Crescent City Confidential

"This book blew my socks off...[*Crescent City Confidential*] ticks all the boxes I've started to expect from Aurora Rey. It is written very well and the characters are extremely well developed; I felt like I was getting to know new friends and my excitement grew with every finished chapter."—*Les Rêveur*

"This book will make you want to visit New Orleans if you have never been. I enjoy descriptive writing and Rey does a really wonderful job of creating the setting. You actually feel like you know the place."—*Amanda's Reviews*

"*Crescent City Confidential* pulled me into the wonderful sights, sounds and smells of New Orleans. I was totally captivated by the city and the story of mystery writer Sam and her growing love for the place and for a certain lady...It was slow burning but romantic and sexy too. A mystery thrown into the mix really piqued my interest."—*Kitty Kat's Book Review Blog*

"*Crescent City Confidential* is a sweet romance with a hint of thriller thrown in for good measure."—*The Lesbian Review*

Built to Last

"Rey's frothy contemporary romance brings two women together to restore an ancient farmhouse in Ithaca, NY...[T]he women totally click in bed, as well as when they're poring over paint chips, and readers will enjoy finding out whether love conquers all."
—*Publishers Weekly*

"*Built to Last* by Aurora Rey is a contemporary lesbian romance novel and a very sweet summer read. I love, love, love the way Ms Rey writes bedroom scenes, and I'm not talking about how she describes the furniture."—*The Lesbian Review*

Autumn's Light

"Aurora Rey is by far one of my favourite authors. She writes books that just get me...Her winning formula is butch women who fall for strong femmes. I just love it. Another triumph from the pen of Aurora Rey. 5 stars."—*Les Rêveur*

Spring's Wake

"*Spring's Wake* has shot to number one in my age-gap romance favorites shelf."—*Les Rêveur*

"The Ptown setting was idyllic and the supporting cast of characters from the previous books made it feel welcoming and homey. The love story was slow and perfectly timed, with a fair amount of heat. I loved it and hope that this isn't the last from this particular series."—*Kitty Kat's Book Review Blog*

"The third standalone in Aurora Rey's Cape End series, *Spring's Wake*, features a feel-good romance that would make a perfect beach read. The Provincetown B&B setting is richly painted, feeling both indulgent and cozy."— *RT Book Reviews*

"*Spring's Wake* by Aurora Rey is charming. This is the third story in Aurora Rey's Cape End romance series and every book gets better. Her stories are never the same twice and yet each one has a uniquely her flavour. The character work is strong and I find it exciting to see what she comes up with next."—*The Lesbian Review*

Summer's Cove

"As expected in a small-town romance, *Summer's Cove* evokes a sunny, light-hearted atmosphere that matches its beach setting... Emerson's shy pursuit of Darcy is sure to endear readers to her, though some may be put off during the moments Darcy winds tightly to the point of rigidity. Darcy desires romance yet is unwilling to disrupt her son's life to have it, and you feel for Emerson when she endeavors to show how there's room in her heart for a family."
—*RT Book Reviews*

school where she wouldn't be allowed to express herself freely was unthinkable to her.

"I didn't want to study and then commit suicide; I knew I couldn't bluff my way through Russian ballet." So I had to come up with another method to generate something wonderful without having to work hard." Stevie merged her love of dancing and preoccupation with popular music by spinning in front of her mirror, putting out routines and stage acts with the assistance of her younger brother, whom she would pay 50 cents to dance with her. Everything Stevie enjoyed and desired for the rest of her life - music, performance, escape, and dressing up (although not as much as tiny brothers) - was coming together. By the time Stevie was 15 years old, in 1963, the Nicks family had relocated again, this time to Los Angeles. If Stevie ever felt nostalgic for her previous bedroom as the moving van neared, her mother, Barbara, would advise her to look forward rather than back. "There's always a better house," she'd reassure her teary-eyed daughter as she returned to the floor she'd danced on and the window she'd gazed out of for the last time.

Stevie's bedroom was crucial to her since she spent so much time there; it was a safe sanctuary for her to read, ponder, and most importantly, dream. Barbara and Jess were protective of their daughter, and she was kept inside far more than the average youngster in the 1960s, but one advantage was that the fantasy world she created in her mind developed powerful enough to affect her future outlook. Despite her awful short-sightedness, she believed completely in wishes and the power of the mind to make things happen, and she sought enchantment in the most mundane aspects of everyday life. Without her spectacles, the world was out of focus, converting a simple naked light bulb into a 'star' and providing her with 'beautiful light shows' whenever she removed her specs. She later pondered if her early experiences with changing misfortune into something beautiful influenced her mystical outlook on everyday life. Stevie Nicks can find the magic in myopia. School would be difficult to adjust to since as soon as Stevie settled in, the family was forced to migrate. Being shy and wanting to meet new people on a regular basis wasn't a good combination, but Stevie had learned a long time ago that if she wanted an easy life, she had to forget about her uneasiness - or at least cover it - and be adaptable and pleasant.

After all, she had to make friends right away or be on her alone for the rest of the year until it was time to move on, and these formative experiences would benefit her later in life. "I learned to get accepted quickly because I didn't have time to waste," she explained to me. "To be snooty for six months until I decided to come down to earth and be a part of everything didn't work at all."

In contrast, Arcadia High School was a "hotsie-totsie, very cliquey, and lots of rich people went there" school. Stevie, on the other hand, was somewhat of an aberration in comparison. Stephanie Nicks stood out amid the trendy jocks and well-groomed debutantes. You could not have missed her. "I dressed kinda crazy and I always had a big straw bag because I wanted to carry everything with me," she went on to say. "People who went to school with me would tell you, 'She was a little crazy, she loved her music, and she was interesting.'" "I believe I piqued everyone's interest."

Stevie may not have won over the popular kids in class to the point of being accepted into their gang, but she felt safe enough at school to show off her singing prowess on a 'father-daughter' night. She and Jess, who also had a strong singing voice, chose to sing the Roger Miller song 'King Of The Road,' which may have been written for AJ. They practised for a week and gave an incredible performance, not least because Stevie burst out laughing seconds after beginning to sing. "I was singing away," she blurted out, "and Stevie was singing away, and she got to laughing, and I got to laughing and I'll be damned if she didn't wet her pants right there on the stage!"

"I got the giggles during the first line, 'Trailer for sale or rent' and I was just hysterical," Stevie said. "He [gave] me this look, like, 'How could you do this to me?'" Wetting yourself in front of your colleagues...This would have been a perfect time to switch schools, but Stevie would stay at Arcadia for another academic year, and it would be a year full of momentous occurrences for Stevie.

1) She would join her first band, The Changing Times, a vocal harmony group modelled after the Mamas and Papas and highly influenced by the West Coast sound.

2) Stevie received permission to begin guitar lessons just before her 16th birthday.

3) She would create her first song.

Barbara and Jess weren't sure if their daughter's strong desire for a guitar was a fleeting interest, so they paid for six weeks of tuition with a Spanish classical guitarist who loaned them a guitar for her to study on. Stevie had classes twice a week, and at the end of the course, his parents were sure that this wasn't a fleeting fad. Because her teacher was moving to Spain to study, he agreed to sell Stevie's miniature classical Goya guitar to Barbara and Jess, who planned to present it to her on her birthday. Stevie adored it (she still has it today) and immediately began writing a song. It was already coming out of her: a ballad about an unrequited teenage love. It was the ideal inspiration for her first song, and as she turned 16, it felt like a rite of passage. Stevie acknowledges the song was "pretty goofy," but it included a chorus, two verses, and an ending. I knew I wanted to be a songwriter from that point forward."

The song was titled 'I've Loved And I've Lost, And I'm Sad But Not Blue,' and it implied that she had accepted that the boy she loved had rejected her and instead chose to go out with a friend. Unfortunately, history would repeat itself 15 years later, with the heartache inspiring a poem, which led to a song. As terrible as it was at times, these difficult times were, in the words of poet Robert Graves, 'compost,' and some exquisite blooms would grow as a result.

Stevie's first real lover was allegedly Dave Young, a quarterback on the school football team, but photographs of him bringing Stevie to senior prom exist, so this sombre ballad is undoubtedly not about him. Another move was on the way, and where the family was going would offer Stevie plenty of opportunities to sing and perform among like-minded people. Jess Nicks' job would eventually take them to San Mateo, California, where Stevie would begin high school in 1966 at Menlo-Atherton High School. She was a 'instant hit,' as Mick Fleetwood put it, finishing second at Homecoming Queen in her first year. Songwriting and poetry had balanced her, giving her the confidence, expressiveness, and poise that distinguished her from many of her awkward adolescent peers. With her beauty, balletic physical elegance, easy charm, and an inner core of resolve, she could accomplish anything. She was also changing her appearance, which would trigger a seismic shift in how she perceived herself. Stevie Nicks eventually converted herself into a mini-rock'n'roll star. "I had my hair streaked at the end of my tenth-grade year and got in a lot of trouble for it," she recounted. "They didn't just streak it blond; they streaked it silver as well." My hair was all white. I was restricted from leaving the house for six weeks. But when I changed my hairstyle, everything changed. "There was no way I was returning."

Stevie was still a 'lovely girl' at this point, despite the horrific hair-streaking incident. She rarely annoyed her parents (except for the occasional temper tantrum - her pouting was legendary), she was serious about her ambition, and she rarely went out. However, she went to one weekly event just to get out of the house: a 'Young Life' church meeting for students. "No one came to church," Stevie admits. It was simply something to do, a venue for young people who enjoyed singing and performing music to hang out on a dreary Wednesday night. Someone drew Stevie's attention at one of these low-key events: a stunning' adolescent kid with curly hair and vivid blue eyes walked in with his guitar, sat down, and began playing 'California Dreaming'.

Stevie, who was immediately taken to him, approached and joined in, singing the Michelle Phillips harmonies she was accustomed to. "He was, I guess, ever so slightly impressed," Stevie explained. The teenager remained composed, but "he did sing another song with me, which let me know he liked it." The two would not see each other again for a while, but they had created a friendship. Lindsey Buckingham was a young guitarist with an expressive singing voice, and Stevie had fallen for him.

Lindsey Buckingham, a year younger than Stevie at school, was a native Californian who grew up in the affluent Bay Area enclave of Atherton. Lindsey, the youngest of three athletic brothers, discovered his love of music rather than sports at a young age, playing along with his brother Jeff's Chuck Berry, Elvis Presley, and Everly Brothers recordings on a plastic Mickey Mouse guitar. Lindsey's parents, who had seen his early potential, would not wait long to acquire him a proper guitar. However, he never took a lesson; the fiercely independent young Lindsey preferred to learn by feel and ear. Lindsey admired folk music and the finger-picking style used on the banjo, which he modelled after The Kingston Trio, a Palo Alto folk group. Lindsey Buckingham was ready to join a band when he was in his mid-teens.

CHAPTER 2
FIRST BAND

The Fritz Rabyne Memorial Band was named after a Menlo-Atherton student as a joke; whether the real Fritz Rabyne, a shy German boy still alive at the time, took this as a compliment is unknown, but his chronic shyness, combined with the sudden popularity of his name, was not a good mix. "He moved away, and we never heard from him again," Fritz co-founder Javier Pacheco stated. "We hardly knew him to begin with!"

The band, eventually nicknamed 'Fritz,' formed in the autumn of 1966 with Jody Moreing on vocals, her cousin Calvin Roper on guitar, Bob Aguirre on drums, Javier Pacheco on keys, and Lindsey himself on bass instead of guitar. He later explained that he disliked the then-"fashionable hard rock approach" on guitar.

Pacheco wrote the majority of the songs, and Fritz practised frequently at Lindsey's house in Atherton. When Moreing, now a well-known singer-songwriter, and Roper had to quit the band to attend college, an opportunity arose to bring in some new blood. Fritz hired guitarist Brian Kane, and when it came to finding a replacement vocalist, the band tried out a few new female singers, but nothing worked. Lindsey, perhaps unsurprisingly, remembers the wonderful girl who volunteered to sing with him over a year ago and how they reached her. Bob Aguirre dug down Stevie's phone number and invited her to a tryout. Despite the fact that not everyone in the band was convinced, Aguirre (most likely referring to Javier Pacheco) claimed, "I knew right away." It was effective. Fritz now had not only a new singer, but also someone who could write new songs, with a more country vibe. Perhaps this is one of the reasons for the disagreements between Javier, who wrote several of the songs, and Stevie. Nonetheless, no one could deny that Stevie possessed something unique about her that signalled success, which was both frightening and promising. Stevie, on the other hand, later stated she "really had no idea what I was getting myself into when I said I would join Fritz." Nonetheless, it would be an ideal training ground.

Fritz and Stevie's first performance together was at Stanford University's Quad. "A big deal," Aguirre told Fleetwood Mac fans at a recent Q&A session. "Stevie did a version of Linda Ronstadt's 'Different Drum' that brought the house down...by popular demand, we had to do it again." "It was written on the wall."

According to Javier Pacheco, the new recruits arrived in late summer 1967, not 1968, as other reports indicate. "Within two or three months," recollects Stevie Nicks, "we were opening for Hendrix, Janis Joplin, and all the San Francisco bands." The connection was fantastic, her voice and appearance were flawless, and the audience adored her. Fritz was no longer a school band, but one of the hottest groups in the Bay Area music industry, with lofty goals. They rehearsed at least four times a week and put in a lot of energy on stage. Stevie had previously shown a knack for the dramatic, 'acting' out her songs and enthralling audiences with her performances. This didn't always go well with the rest of the band.

Pacheco stated that, while Stevie's emotional renditions were noteworthy, it all sounded like a "big put on," particularly when they played the Buffy Sainte Marie song "Codeine." "Stevie doubled up and acted out withdrawal pains while she sang it," he said. "I used to become upset about it...It was her side of the stage. Stevie, on the other hand, persisted, and this was constantly recognized. It caused them to feel something. However, she can also move you with a simple country song.

Pacheco says that he believed Stevie was a shrinking violet who "couldn't cut it" when she first joined the group and was getting her bearings. "Once it became clear that she would be staying with the band, I resigned myself to working around her vocal strengths and weaknesses," he later remarked cynically. But, as resigned as he was, he would constantly tease her. "Stevie became the victim, and I was the big bad wolf," he went on to say. "I was critical of Stevie, but her songs did move me, [and] her first Fritz songs have stayed with me."

Around the same time Stevie was doing her best to put up with Javier Pacheco's humiliations, on the other side of the Atlantic, 5,437 miles away in London, guitar prodigy Peter Green was forming the British blues band Fleetwood Mac. Green was a well-known member of John Mayall's Bluesbreakers, and he chose the name for his new band by combining the surnames of the drummer, Mick Fleetwood, and the bassist, John McVie, both of whom had previously played with the Bluesbreakers. Much was expected of the new lineup, but only the most bold clairvoyants could have predicted Fleetwood Mac and Fritz's future connection.

Stevie would wonder why she stayed in Fritz when being the only female amid a group of musos became tedious. But, in the years to come, she'd look back and realise everything had gone exactly as it should have. "It was preparation for Fleetwood Mac," she explained. She also set the ground rules early on: she was the singer. She too was a lady. There would be no hard lifting, assistance with equipment transport, or unloading the van. "I always wanted to be a lead singer." "I didn't want to carry a 21-pound Les Paul," she stated.

Stevie's parents were worried that she should have some employable skills - she was a bright young woman capable of doing so many things - and while Barbara and Jess adored Fritz and were always supportive of Stevie's ambitions, they also wanted her to complete her education. "'I absolutely believe you're going to be a singer and a famous songwriter,' my mother said. But, just in case, I'll need you to learn typing and shorthand. And if you attend college, we will cover all of your fees.' So I went. I believe you should get the best education possible before deciding whether you want to be a full-fledged entrepreneur and space cadet. However, if you are required to care for someone or keep anything together, you must have learned something." Stevie would also go to San Jose State University to study Speech Communication. Lindsey, who majored in art, would join her the next year.

Unlike Moreing, Stevie remained with the band after college, even if it meant commuting every week to gigs and rehearsals. She couldn't commit to as many rehearsals as she used to, which upset some of her colleagues, who practised for hours every day but had to deal with questions about the band "with the little brownish-blondish haired girl..."

Stevie would be watching not only the stars, but also some of the more fashionable members of the audience. During Joplin's set, Stevie was drawn to a woman in the audience. "I saw this girl in the audience wearing a mauvy pink chiffon skirt and very high cream suede boots," Stevie recounted. "She was gorgeous." "Her hair was kind of a Gibson Girl - she had some pink ribbons - and I thought that's it." Layers swathed the woman, a mix of bouffant Victorian elegance, free-flowing gypsy charm, and exquisitely tattered street urchin style. Stevie didn't mind confessing that she 'wanted to be her,' and she would carry these images in her head, hunting for goods at markets and antique stores that fit the image she wanted to create. One day, she'd be able to have that look custom-made for her, but in the meanwhile, she'd have to make do with off-the-rack clothing. That didn't mean she couldn't dress like a legend.

Stevie had done her research; she knew that Janis and Grace shopped at the hip Velvet Underground boutique in San Francisco, so she would stride through the streets on a Saturday afternoon, her Goya guitar slung over one shoulder, and kit herself out right there, just like her heroines. Bell bottoms, tunics, evening gowns, lovely fabrics...The boutique was small, but it had everything Stevie needed to alter herself, and with money she'd earned from a part-time job working in a clothing store, she'd "truly splurge..."In these clothes, I'd carry my guitar and walk like a rock star - there was something about my posture and the ballet I'd taken, and I'd be swathing through crowds of people thinking, 'Do you know who I am?'" she chuckles. "I truly believed it. It's like that thing: if you create it, they will come. 'I'm going to be a big star,' I thought. Soon.' "I thought you could plant the seed in people's minds." Stevie's days of ingenuity were long gone. She was reinventing herself as a rock goddess, and it was only a matter of time until the rest of the world caught up and began worshipping her.

Because of the lucrative support slots Fritz was playing in San Francisco, it wasn't long before they were getting the notice of managers and agents who saw their great potential. Not just Stevie and Lindsey were ambitious; the entire group was eager to succeed, and they were quickly signed by a new manager, David Forest. Forest was as determined as they were; he went from running his own business to working with Creative Management Associates in

Los Angeles, and he fought tirelessly to get the band a record deal. The road to rock'n'roll glory is never easy, and while Stevie and Lindsey knew Los Angeles was the place to be, the rest of the band didn't, preferring 'groovy San Francisco' to the 'plastic' City of Angels. The strain was beginning to show, and the conflicting objectives within Fritz were getting more difficult to reconcile. Lindsey no longer wanted to play bass, Brian preferred blues, and, as Javier later admitted, "we were being manipulated by outside forces." He believed Forest 'dragged' the band to LA because he "wanted to continue to control and/or profit from the group." Dave kept Bill Graham's interest in managing the group from us, so Forest convinced us that LA was our only feasible alternative."

But this was not the only reason Fritz broke up after five years of hard work and musical apprenticeship,' and what drew two-fifths of the band to Los Angeles. According to producer Keith Olsen, who was then a starving engineer in Los Angeles, the agent Todd Shipman was "trying to get traction for this band." "[Shipman] began calling all of the A-level producers, asking if they'd be interested in seeing them live in San Jose." When everyone turned him down, he went to the B-level producers - you can see where this is heading - and nobody wanted to go with him. So he went to the C-level, and, well, they weren't interested. So he went to the D-list, which included my name. "'Sure, free ticket to San Jose!' I said. I had no idea they were going to pick me up in a band van with no seats. I got to sit in the back with the drums and assist set up...I was young and didn't give a damn. But when I watched the band that night, I thought to myself, 'There's something unique here...' Lindsey and Stevie had this colour when they sang together...Those voices were supposed to harmonise."

Keith had a gut feeling that Stevie and Lindsey didn't require the rest of the band to succeed. He did, however, persuade Fritz to go to Van Nuys, Los Angeles, to record a demo with him at the now-famous (if somewhat filthy) Sound City studio on Cabrito Road on a quiet Sunday morning. It was exciting to be asked, and when they arrived at the unassuming-looking studio, the band's trepidation was compounded by a minor hiccup: the locks had been changed since Keith had last recorded there. Not all was lost. Keith was tenacious.

"We broke into the studio by removing the door." We entered, left one side of the door open, and recorded. That is understandable.

It was their first time in a decent studio, and the resulting demo was plainly wrong but yet strong. However, after hearing the song following the session, Olsen realised that while he enjoyed it, "something wasn't right." The ensemble contained too many problems. I hate thinking about or talking about it now because they were such good friends, but I told Lindsey and Stevie, 'I'd love to continue working with you, but I believe you'd perform better as a couple.' And, of course, this had devastating consequences. These were the men they'd played with, and I was suggesting that they disband the band; a terrible idea, but reality sometimes requires it. I was upfront and honest, and they said, 'Yeah, we'll think about it,' before driving away."

Keith's conscience can rest easy, for this was not the main reason for their separation in 1971. The band was bickering more than ever, with everyone wanting to go in separate directions, but this tantalising glimpse of a possible future for Stevie and Lindsey would certainly be the tipping moment. All you had to do was listen to the words of Stevie's songs from that era to observe how things were changing. Javier Pacheco described one of Stevie's songs as "right on the mark." The lyrics read, "There's a profound sense of a weird kind of love..." Like a divorce after it's over. She was referring to Fritz's imminent death. In 1970, we were writing love and breakup songs for each other. "This did not start with the Mac."

Stevie and Lindsey could have convinced Keith that they would discuss what he had said, but there was little to ponder about; their fantasy was becoming a reality, and Fritz was already unravelling. But Keith had not only started the Buckingham Nicks' musical career, but he also appeared to have facilitated their courtship by mistake. After Fritz's session at Sound City, Stevie and Lindsey headed to the rustic yet rock n roll-themed Tropicana Motel on Sunset Strip to discuss the possibilities, but the conversation rapidly veered into something else.

"Why it happened between me and Lindsey was because we were so sad that we had to tell the three guys in the band that nobody wanted them, only us," Stevie explained to Fred Shruers of Rolling Stone. "It just happened."

Stevie and her collaborator-turned-boyfriend, much to her parents' dismay, were planning to drop out of college and relocate to Los Angeles, following in the footsteps of so many others. Stevie's parents were devastated by her decision to abandon her valued education, but her decision to live with a musical lover was almost unbearable. She used to be so lovely...

When a surprise occurred, the couple was nearly ready to move. Lindsey's health had deteriorated, although he had tried to deal with it. What looked to be a simple case of influenza was actually a severe case of mononucleosis (glandular fever), a painful and debilitating sickness that leaves the person with little alternative but to lie flat and do nothing. Lindsey's main goal now was to rest in bed at his parents' place and avoid boredom. This was especially tough for Lindsey, who was incredibly creative but lacked the stamina to lift his head for three months. There were just five TV stations to choose from as well.

Stevie, who usually hung out in the Buckinghams' living room, did everything she could to keep Lindsey entertained, bringing him food, playing records, telling him stories, and generally trying to cheer him up. The experience of having to care for Lindsey while their relationship was still in its early stages deepened their bond even more. She "didn't mother him," recalls Keith Olsen, who remembers Lindsey's difficult time (and is especially sympathetic having suffered with mono himself). "She just poured her heart out to him.""It was such a heartfelt dedication." Lindsey ordered that they study 'form' by listening to the Everly Brothers, the Kingston Trio, and the Beatles. Stevie would have preferred to listen to Aretha Franklin, Diana Ross, and Joni Mitchell instead (Mitchell's 1970 album Ladies Of The Canyon had a particularly strong influence on Nicks), but she followed Lindsey's firm supervision until she 'burned out'.

Lindsey, still lying down, implored Stevie to pass him his guitar someday. At this point, he experienced a shift that would forever change the way he played. "He didn't have enough strength to strum," Keith explains. "All he had was the strength to use his fingers." Consider how he plays the guitar; it's entirely due to mono. Because of his illness, he evolved into a brilliant super player with his own distinct style. It was a semi-flamenco finger-picking style, but he was using the backs of his fingers very swiftly. As a result, he was able to formulate his soloing strategy." Lindsey had always admired bluegrass guitarists and banjo players' finger-picking styles as a child, and this, combined with his often frantic self-taught technique, helped him create an entirely new sound that contrasted with Stevie's mellifluous voice as she harmonised with his more urgent, plaintive tenor. Lindsey had never given Fritz music, but something had changed. Lindsey's health eventually improved, much to Stevie's relief, and her love and support were reciprocated with the creation of a new song called 'Stephanie,' a sweet, romantic instrumental. Another song he wrote during this exhausting period was considerably harsher in tone. 'I'm So Afraid,' later a popular Fleetwood Mac song, is a brutal glimpse into Lindsey's terrified, neurotic mind, as well as an angry, despairing depiction of how he must have felt physically. 'I'll never change, I'll never change/ I'm so afraid of how I feel...'

Lows were balanced by highs, and as Lindsey's strength improved, so did their fortune: Lindsey had lately been handed a significant inheritance by an aunt he had never met, and he used the money to buy an Ampex four-track tape recorder 'the size of a washing machine' as soon as he could. Morris Buckingham, Stevie's father, owned a coffee business near the Cow Palace in Palo Alto, and he let Stevie and Lindsey practice in the warehouse after the workers had gone home for the night.

Almost every night, the couple would write and work in that 'scary' chamber from 9pm till daybreak. "It was so scary that we locked ourselves in the room and didn't go out because it was a big warehouse," Stevie said. "If we heard things, we would just stay in there and keep the door locked."

Aside from the creepiness, the acoustics were fantastic, and it was here that Lindsey not only taught himself how to use the machine and achieve exactly the sound he wanted, but also where the duo recorded their first demos as Buckingham Nicks, with the intention of returning to LA and landing a record deal. 'Frozen Love' was one of several songs written during this period of hothousing, and as Mick Fleetwood subsequently commented, it was during this period of hothousing that Lindsey established his meticulous producer's approach, which he would become known for later in his career. All of those nights spent labouring in Mo Buckingham's massive coffee plant will soon pay off. Stevie and Lindsey loaded the four-track into the back of their rusty car, drove back to LA, and knocked on Keith Olsen's door.

"Lindsey placed it in my home and said, 'Listen to this.'" I was completely taken aback. Oh my goodness. "I took those demos and started going around selling them," Keith explains. Olsen already knew Stevie and Lindsey's voices were great together, but they also had the music that would propel them to the next level. The dust of gold.

Lindsey and Stevie signed up with Keith's company, Pogo Logo Productions, and promised to split the profits evenly. "It was the good old days," Keith adds. Buckingham Nicks clearly had an album's worth of lovely, strange tunes in them; the only thing standing in their way was a paucity of funds. This would not be an issue for long. Keith approached David Shackler, former head of A&R at major label Polydor, while pushing the recordings around. Stevie and Lindsey's demos captivated Shackler right away. In turn, he would sign Buckingham Nicks to Anthem Records, a Polydor subsidiary. The mission had begun.

Stevie and Lindsey temporarily moved in with Keith Olsen in his 'small house on the hill' in Van Nuys while they settled in and looked for their own property. When their own car broke down again, Olsen generously let them borrow his cherished new Corvette. To say the least, he regretted his decision. He may now laugh about it, but...

"I was leaving for New York to mix a James Gang show in Central Park." I had this little Corvette with maybe 350 miles on it, a stick shift, and I needed to go down to Domenic Troiano, the guitarist. Back in the Valley, we all met." Keith got out of his car to wait for the limousine to transport them to the airport with the rest of the band, only to see Stevie emerge from the house 'with her robe and fluffy slippers, hair in a towel.' She clearly needs the use of a vehicle. Stevie had never driven a manual transmission before, but that didn't stop her. Keith and the James Gang watched her as she tried to make her way down the drive.

"She finally gets it going, but it's making all these noises," Keith recalls. "Roy [Kenner], the James Gang's singer, looks at me and says, 'You'll never see that car again.'" 'Oh no, she'll get the feel of it, she'll succeed,' I said. That's what she did. However, the automobile would not. When Keith and the James Gang landed in New York, disaster had already struck. Keith entered his hotel room to discover a light flickering on his phone, and a message waiting for him: "It's Lindsey." Place a call to your home. It's somewhat of a crisis."

"I dial my house, and Lindsey picks up," Keith says. "The first question I ask is, 'Is everyone okay?' And he answers, 'Yeah...'"But your car is in your next-door neighbour's bedroom." We are on a steep climb. Stevie had applied the emergency brake, left it in neutral, clicked, and departed the vehicle. It started to roll, and about 40 minutes later, a man knocked on the door. 'Do you have a gold-coloured automobile?' 'Well, sort of.' Stevie replies. 'It is in my bedroom,' he explained. It literally fell from the cliff and through his bedroom ceiling. "It was the most incredible thing."

Olsen was definitely a sympathetic and supportive presence in their lives, but Stevie and Lindsey's decision to move out was certainly for the best, especially since they would soon be working together every day at the studio. Keith introduced the couple to Richard Dashut, a dark-haired, bearded outsider with a passion for British blues bands like Fleetwood Mac, the Yardbirds, and the Bluesbreakers, as well as a nasty glint in his eye. He started as a caretaker at Sound City, but after a week, he was promoted to assistant engineer under Olsen. Stevie and Lindsey got along well with him, and they quickly found themselves renting a home in North Hollywood near Universal Studios. Stevie met musician Tom Moncrieff through Dashut, who would occasionally stay with them and become Stevie's long-term lover for many years. Nicks and Buckingham's relationship was equal parts intense loyalty and even fiercer creative rivalry, elements that make their live performances so engaging to this day. Decades after their divorce, it appears that the public continues to root for Buckingham and Nicks, despite the reality that their love will never be realised. It is without a doubt rock's largest and most difficult romance. Stevie and Lindsey could not have guessed how popular their stormy relationship would become in the coming years. They were simply trying to make ends meet, write enough songs for the album, and remain in love.

But the course had been determined, Sound City was overjoyed to have them, and the record agreement had been finalised. The label provided an advance to cover studio time and accommodation costs for everyone involved, and they were finally getting a "taste of the big time," as Stevie put it.

Keith Olsen's friend Richard Dashut wasn't the only one who helped Buckingham Nicks make their debut album memorable; Tom Moncrieff, initially on guitar and later on bass, as well as a guitarist named Waddy Wachtel, with whom Olsen had worked since the late 1960s and who later secured a deal with Polydor subsidiary Anthem himself, would also join the band. Keith was excited to bring together Waddy ("another of those super-players who is so creative," as Keith describes him) with Buckingham Nicks, knowing that his playing would compliment their songs. They connected immediately, with Waddy bonding with Stevie over Dolly Parton and Lindsey bonding over marijuana. The Buckingham Nicks family was complete, and they were ready to record, thanks to fellow Pogologo signee Jorge Calderon on percussion.

Buckingham Nicks' recording in the grungy but exhilarating surroundings of Sound City made it all worthwhile; the musicians relished spending time together and believed they were creating something wonderful. Stevie and Lindsey did not take the opportunity to perform with musicians such as Tom, Jorge, and Waddy for granted. Furthermore, they were making history: the renowned Sound City console (now owned by Dave Grohl) was "the first big giant Neve console in America," according to Keith. "I insisted on purchasing this console because I owned a piece of Sound City at the time." I recorded 'Crying In The Night' with Buckingham Nicks the first time we plugged it in and turned it on.""That was the first thing I recorded there."

The album was scheduled to be released in September 1973, with the song 'Don't Let Me Down Again' serving as the lead single. The record would be dedicated to Stevie's grandfather, AJ, but the cover would not be appropriate for him. Stevie spent the remaining $111 on a gorgeous, "very sexy" white blouse to wear for the cover, knowing that the picture shoot was approaching. However, it would be unnecessary. Waddy suggested that his brother Jimmy, who was now an art director, photograph the album artwork, and it was agreed that Stevie could wear the garment she was so proud of in some of the shots. Stevie was convinced that she would 'win,' that they would love the blouse and how stunning she looked in it; pure heavenly hippy chic. Midway into the session, "one of the photographers came over and said, 'OK, it's time to take off the blouse.'"

The cover was going to show a bare-chested Buckingham and Nicks in sad black and white. Stevie loathed the idea and even sobbed during the shot. These naked images were "the most terrifying moment of my entire life," she later claimed, but Lindsey was unfazed, reprimanding her for being childish and unpleasant. But Stevie promised herself that she would never allow herself to be compromised again. Instead, she'd be as appealing as heck 'under 18 pounds of chiffon and velvet' while still keeping her mystique.

When Stevie's family saw the cover, they were terrified. "It was a big shock, let me tell you," Stevie's mother, Barbara, told The Arizona Republic. "I just told her, 'We'll have to think about this before showing it to dad.'" Stevie didn't want him to see it. But she was young at the time and had been coaxed into it." According to Stevie, AJ Nicks was not impressed with the album, though seeing his granddaughter allegedly naked on a record cover may have been too much for him. Stevie, on the other hand, believed there was more than a trace of bitterness in AJ Nicks' reaction to small Stevie's big moment, as well as a sense of regret about what may have been had his own journey as a musician gone differently.

To make matters worse, the record was ultimately a flop (save for Birmingham, Alabama, where it allegedly garnered a lot of radio play). It did not go gold; Polydor dropped it, and Buckingham Nicks was immediately dropped. Stevie and Lindsey were heartbroken.

"It was hard when you practise that hard and you sound that good and everybody tells you that you should be doing something else," Stevie explained to Creem. "You want to say something like, 'Obviously, we're not from the same planet, because I didn't sit with this guy for five years and sing like this for you to tell me that nothing we do is commercial.'" Lindsey and I couldn't understand how we could sing such a beautiful song and have no one enjoy it. It was as if they were saying, 'We don't belong here, and no one understands us.

But it was time to put the melancholy aside and return to work. Normal, or rather weird, service was resumed; writing and practising continued, Lindsey smoked another doobie, and Stevie got a new waitressing job at Clementine's, an expensive Los Angeles restaurant with a 1920s theme, paying $1.50 per hour. There was a lot of running around -- Stevie claims she was in the best physical shape of her life -- and the waitresses had to dress up as flappers, which the roguish Richard Dashut found funny. Stevie would "try to find ways to make Hamburger Helper different..." for dinner, which was not so funny when Stevie returned home to find that a stoned Lindsey had put her electric skillet on the stove, "and cooked the Hamburger Helper in the electric skillet, which meant we had no more electric skillet, and no more Hamburger Helper..."

Stevie would occasionally bring home a slice of pizza for herself and Lindsey to share, providing just enough nourishment to get through the night. "I'd get home from my waitress job, we'd have dinner, and then we'd start working at nine o'clock at night until two or three o'clock in the morning." Then I'd go to bed, get up, and he'd work on the music, while I went to work as a waitress."

Buckingham was engaged by Don Everly of the Everly Brothers to play guitar and sing harmony during a tour in the fall of 1974. The Everly Brothers split up midway through a concert at Knott's Berry Farm amusement park on July 14, 1973. Don was too drunk to sing all of the lyrics, resulting in significant gaps in the middle of songs. Phil Everly slammed his guitar on the stage halfway through the second set, signalling his departure from the band. Don became sober, relocated to Nashville, and formed his own band with Robert Wachtel on guitar and Warren Zevon on keyboards. He hoped against hope that his debut solo album, Sunset Towers, would be as successful as "Wake Up, Little Suzie" and "Love Hurts." Wachtel was unable to go on tour owing to other engagements, so he recommended Buckingham. The rehearsals began in Aspen,

Colorado. To save money, members of the Everly "entourage" parked at Crystal Zevon's parents' home. Nicks and Buckingham arrived in their Toyota from Los Angeles, and after the rest of the band left, Nicks lingered at Crystal's invitation. She intended to write music during her time away from Clementine's. The tour was a disappointment and ended early. Buckingham returned to Aspen with a bad attitude, according to Nicks. He was really upset with me; he took Ginnie the poodle and the car and abandoned me in Aspen on the day the Greyhound buses were on strike. I had a bus pass because my father was the president of Greyhound, and I could travel wherever I chose. I replied, "Fine, take the car and the dog, I have a bus pass." I also got strep throat. He drives away, I walk in, and the radio says, "Greyhound buses are on strike throughout the United States." I am going, yet I am stuck. So I called my folks to get out of Colorado, and they reluctantly sent me a plane ticket since they didn't understand why I was up there in the first place. So I accompanied him back to Los Angeles in October, around Halloween, and two months later, Fleetwood Mac called on New Year's Eve. She wrote a song about her feelings before her parents gave her the vacation, and it wasn't all about her boyfriend. Her grandfather died in August, her father was diagnosed with heart disease, and both he and her mother intimated that living with Buckingham and pursuing a career in music might not be the greatest option.

The song "Landslide," which she wrote in Aspen, is a classic—truly beautiful. The words, like snow, conceal and reveal, obscuring individual details while revealing larger patterns. The song describes what is beneath the surface. The narrator describes the seasons of life, as well as how the past is reflected in the present and future. She describes sinking into a panorama of truths obscured by the outside world. The narrator looks out a window at the mountain and imagines climbing it just to sink back into the snow. As the title suggests, the music descends, with diminishing intervals for the word "down" narrating her emotional descent. Fear of change is conveyed by a harmonic shift in which the guitar mutates beneath repeated lines of text, altering how she transmits the words but not their essence. G minor is inserted into the texture, followed by G minor 7, which complicates the chord and captures the intricacies that come with expertise. The nature of love is questioned in the verses, with the answer found and dreaded in the chorus—hence the minor undertow to the major. The bridge between verses is palindromic, with the sound moving ahead and then backward, from present to past and future. The lyrics address "the child within [her] heart," and in the chorus she offers the essential sad truth that "children get older." The book is, of course, about physically ageing and maturing throughout time. "Landslide" vividly illustrates the perils of maturation. The refrain, "the landslide will bring you down," builds before collapsing at the end, and the song ends with the first verse repeated and a fermata-like pause in the voice before the last drop. The conclusion is a declaration: some events are beyond our control, such as ruined relationships, years of regret, and slush that contaminates the snow. Seasons change, and we all wonder what we can bear, yet the annular fillip in the guitar and the down-to-up pitch reversals suggest a certain fortitude—a way to ski the slopes. The song is easy to sing since the melody, like life, tolerates imperfection and encourages adaptability. Its status as a classic reflects the "persistence" of its "sentiment," to use the title of Mitchell Morris' excellent book about songs from the 1970s that people love unashamedly and guiltlessly (if a little sheepishly). Covers are provided by The Smashing Pumpkins (surprisingly reverent), the Chicks (cutting the wounded heart of bluegrass), and Stacey Kent (jazzified, with delightfully precise language). The majority of the affection is focused at songs heard as a child, and growing old with them while new songs are made for the next generation is a sad and joyful reminder that, as Morris writes, "we become history along with the things we have chosen to love." "Landslide" is about the exquisite tragedy of becoming history.

"rhiannon"

"Rhiannon," the companion song that defined Nicks' career, was written around the same time. It is supposed to have come about as a result of bibliomancy, or seeing the future on a random page in a book. On this occasion, Nicks read Mary Bartlet Leader's Triad (1973), "a stupid little paperback," she adds, "that I found somewhere at somebody's house, lying on the couch" around Halloween. Nicks has also indicated that she purchased the novel in an airport, probably while returning to Los Angeles from Aspen. In any case, the plot of this surprisingly appealing page-turner is as follows: Branwen, a freelance writer, has recently lost her infant boy to Sudden Infant Death Syndrome. She and her husband, Alan, who occasionally travels for business, are seeking for a new beginning, so they purchase a derelict home on a lake to renovate. Branwen is tormented by another childhood loss: the accidental death of her evil cousin, Rhiannon, whom she locked in an antique freezer while playing hide-and-seek. Rhiannon suffocated when the rusty handle snapped and she was unable to escape. Branwen's house evokes that loss: speaking tubes connecting the rooms mumble Rhiannon's name, and Branwen, who believes Rhiannon has returned from the dead to control her, begins to disintegrate, blacking out often. Then Branwen discovers she is pregnant—or is Rhiannon? Branwen gets diagnosed with multiple personality disorder by her physician. Branwen gives birth, and her husband adopts the kid after she is imprisoned with her alter ego in an asylum. "At worst," she says, "I'll have to stay in an institution... for the rest of my life." But I've closed the door on Rhiannon. She can't escape as long as I'm alive. However, if there is someone—someone with remarkable insight—the world may be able to defeat Rhiannon. I know one thing: the curtain that divides this life from the unknown beyond must be lifted someday, for that veil, our ignorance, serves as both our shield and her weapon.

The novel's epigraph alludes to the title's "triad": Branwen represents Branwen, the daughter of Llr, the Britons' queen. Branwen's marriage to the Irish king has negative consequences for both countries. The second member of the trio is Caradog ap Bran, Branwen's cousin, and the third is Faraon Dandde, a king whose son was murdered.

According to the novel and its epigraph, Leader was familiar with the Mabinogion, a collection of mediaeval Welsh traditions, though not in their original form but through popular retellings. These eleven Middle Welsh prose tales, discovered in fourteenth-century manuscripts, appear to be from at least the twelfth century. They were courtly entertainments having a moral purpose, from diverse ages and conditions. Four of the stories are related and known as the Four Branches of the Mabinogi, which is a scribal version of the nineteenth-century collective word Mabinogion. Branwen is the primary figure in the Mabinogi's Second Branch, which recounts her ill-fated marriage to the King of Ireland, orchestrated by her brother

Bendigeidfran (Bran the Blessed). Branwen is imprisoned and brutalised in Ireland; she teaches a starling to speak and sends it across the Irish Sea to her brother, who invades Ireland to free her, evoking the Leader's hero's incarceration in the institution. Nicks utilised the image of the starling ("And the starling flew for days") not in "Rhiannon" but in another song, "Sara."

Rhiannon, the main character in the Mabinogi's First Branch, is a heavenly woman who marries Pwyll, the mortal ruler of Dyfed (South Wales). Rhiannon is associated with three songbirds who follow her in both the Mabinogion and the Welsh Triads, a collection of late-mediaeval story themes (which no doubt inspired Leader's novel Triad); mythographers have also linked her to the Gaulish horse deity Epona. Nicks became obsessed with the name Rhiannon and claimed to have learned more about the figure's past:

After finishing the song, I learned that Rhiannon was the goddess of horses and the creator of birds. Rhiannon's three birds sang melodies, and when there was a disagreement, she would come in on horseback. This is the complete Welsh translation of the Mabinogion, their mythology book. When she arrived, you'd sort of blank out, only to wake up to find the threat gone, the three birds flying away, and this tiny singing. So there was, indeed, a Rhiannon song. I was absolutely unaware of all of this. Nicks read the four-volume novelization of the Mabinogion by renowned fantasy writer Evangeline Walton (1907-96), which was sent to her by a fan. The second volume, The Song of Rhiannon, was published in 1972. Walton chooses an aggregate because the roots of the hero-goddess are not stated in the Mabinogion or Triads. Rhiannon is the gorgeous night queen, moon goddess, and a representation of female independence, magic, and power. She rides a swift white horse, as in the original First Branch of the Mabinogi, while songbirds circle her head. Pwyll marries her and has a child. In Walton's modern retelling of the ancient tale, the god she was supposed to have married exacts revenge by framing her for the child's death. Nicks visited Walton at her "totally Rhiannon" home in Tucson in 1977 or 1978. The author was in her mid-seventies and had an ailment that caused her skin to turn purple. Walton went on to tell Nicks "about her life and how she had been entranced by the name, just like I had." It's fascinating because her last work was released in 1974, the same year I wrote

Rhiannon. So it's as if her work was done and mine began." Walton granted Nicks the rights to a Rhiannon movie for free. She has composed music for it, but it has not yet been produced. The lyrics of the song indicate that Nicks knows more about the Rhiannon story than he discloses. Perhaps she divined it, or she came to the Mabinogion through Leader and Walton's writings earlier than she admits. The statement "She rules her life like a bird in flight" appears to be influenced by the Mabinogion, while the question "Will you ever win?" is reminiscent of Triad's ending. The song's similes and metaphors are distinctly Nicks': Rhiannon is both "a cat in the dark" and "the darkness." In "Rhiannon," the legend's starling is turned into a skylark, accompanied by an erotic metaphor to a nighttime bell ringing. "Dreams unwind / Love's a state of mind" also highlights Nicks' distinctive voice. Nicks said that the song's structure came to her in a matter of minutes, as if an old voice was channelling through her. A minor chord opposing F, raised to C: the enchantress came to represent both uplift and the soothing impact of music. Nicks sent over the tape draft to Buckingham. He found it by the coffee pot, with a note reading, "Here is a new song." You can create it, but you cannot change it." He didn't, and it became a hit, catapulting her to a new level as an artist and giving her creative opportunities to which she would return repeatedly. As 1974 approached 1975, fame appeared on the horizon, or just beyond it. Mick Fleetwood heard Buckingham Nicks at Sound City in December. Nicks was there that day, demoing "Rhiannon" for a potential Buckingham Nicks sequel. Despite the fact that he apparently saw her, she was not Fleetwood's main focus. He was more interested in the epic guitar solo on "Frozen Love," which Olsen played for him, as well as two other songs off the album, one by Emitt Rhodes and one by Aretha Franklin. Fleetwood signed a deal with Olsen after hearing his production work on the albums, which included orchestrating acoustic and electric guitars and enhancing bottom end registers. However, on New Year's Eve, Fleetwood called Olsen and informed him that guitarist Bob Welch had lately quit Fleetwood Mac. He remembered "Frozen Love" and asked Olsen about Buckingham's availability.

"So, that fellow in that band you played me—would you see if that guy would like to join my band?" "Well, they're going to come as a set," I explained. Because they're each obsessed with their own thing, and the only way to convince them to stop is to bring them both on." "Well, maybe that will work," he says. "Could you see if you can persuade them to join my band?"

I cancel my plans for New Year's Eve [1974], bring my girlfriend, and we head to Stevie and Lindsey's apartment. "Hey, Happy New Year," I began, bringing over the typical bottle of horrible champagne, before asking, "Can we talk?" Mick Fleetwood wants you to be a member of Fleetwood Mac.

Buckingham was stunned when Nicks indicated interest, stating, "Oh, no, no—I couldn't possibly play anything as good as Peter Green did." "How am I going to get up there and play 'The Green Manalishi'?"—a mescaline-fueled tangle of powerful guitar effects and haunting vocals. However, by the end of the evening, after five hours of lobbying, Olsen had convinced the pair to give Fleetwood Mac a try, with no obligation to perform "Manalishi," if only for a few weeks. The story evolves alongside the teller. Buckingham first heard from Fleetwood in Washington, DC, near the end of the Everly tour—a two-week engagement at the Cellar Door in Georgetown, a small venue that attracted a variety of top-tier talent: "As we walk down the street, Lindsey announces, 'I just got a call from Fleetwood Mac, and they want me to join their band.'" 'Are you nuts, Lindsey?' I questioned. You make $450 per week, your bills are paid, and you work with celebrities." "Why would you want to do that?" Fleetwood Mac, which was rarely charting and bleeding people, appeared doomed for obscurity.

According to Stephen Davis, Nicks bought Fleetwood Mac CDs and thought she and Buckingham had something to give. Buckingham, on the other hand, halted. "Listen, Stevie, a hundred fucking people have passed through Fleetwood Mac."It's like a meat grinder"—a reference to the traumatic departures of Welch, founding guitarist Green, who was diagnosed with schizophrenia; Jeremy Spencer, who joined the Children of God cult; and Danny Kirwan for professional and personal reasons, including drunken altercations with the others. "We're doing this," Nicks says to Davis. "I'm tired of being a waitress!"

In January 1975, Fleetwood's assistant Judy Wong organised an encounter at El Carmen, a 1929-founded taqueria on West Third Street that still claims to have the best margaritas in Los Angeles. Mick warned Christine McVie ahead of time, "Chris, if you don't like [Stevie], then it's not going to happen." It was critical because I had never performed in a band with another girl before. So we convened to eat Mexican food. First and foremost, I was intrigued by Lindsey's expression when he walked through the door—I thought to myself, Wow, this guy is a god. Stevie strolled in, giggling, so cute and little, and I instantly liked her. She has a lovely chuckle and an excellent sense of humour. So, toward the conclusion of the evening, I said, "Mick, let's do this."

Imagine this scene: Stevie walks from Clementine's to El Carmen dressed in Gibson Girl vintage, removing long gold hair from her eyes. She takes Lindsey's hand, the musician's musician, blue-eyed and dressed in pants and a flowing shirt, with a moustache, goatee, and a mound of black curly hair. He has already met Christine, a cigarette-breathed, dirty blond, casually dressed in a blouse and denim, both proper and profane in speech; and her jocular, defiantly unsober husband, John, dressed, as Nicks told Ann Powers of NPR, in "shorts, which is what he wore for 25 years, and tennies and a white hat and a little vest." Outside, a white Cadillac with a "glunk glunk" sounds comes up, and out pops Mick is tall, thin, bearded, and dressed like a fop's alley regular. An evening of margaritas (served far past midnight at El Carmen) and laughter cut through any sense of desperation: the senior musicians hoped for another recharge, while the younger wanted a second chance to make it. Nicks and Buckingham remained together for another month, performing four more times in Alabama, the state that, by chance, appreciated them the most. On January 28, they appeared at the Birmingham Fairgrounds, followed by Morgan Auditorium in Tuscaloosa, Jacksonville State University, and Birmingham's Municipal Auditorium, where they had previously performed on August 25, 1974. Buckingham dominated, and during his guitar fantasies, Nicks occasionally left the stage to take a sip of wine. William Alford, a University of Alabama electrical engineering student, recorded the Tuscaloosa concert on reel-to-reel tape using the console. "Lola" sounds great; it's tighter, quicker, and more upbeat than the album version. Nicks also unveiled "Rhiannon." Alford's tape is one of two bootleg versions of the Alabama Run song. Nicks told the 600-person Tuscaloosa audience that "Rhiannon" was inspired by a novel about "a lady with two personalities," and that he "simply had to make a song about it." She's unusual, however... I hope you appreciate it because it's absolutely different." She laughs and turns to the band, adding, "And don't play it too fast." The band plays it too fast. Nicks announced in Jacksonville, with "her hair falling in a long, tangled heap of curls... sometimes serious... almost demonic at times," that she and Buckingham had joined another group. When she said its name, the audience booed before briefly cheering. Polydor had lost faith in her, she told the Birmingham after Dark entertainment guide. Just as her father's relocation propelled him to the top, joining Fleetwood Mac would allow her to advance several stages further:

It would take us years to earn the same reputation they do. And Warner Bros. is a huge fan of Fleetwood Mac. They aren't a monster or a massive act, but they routinely sell more albums than the previous time. They'll put us on a big huge tour where we'll play to everyone. And they're really kind folks, so we decided it'd be a great learning experience. They can assist us, and we can assist them, so it will be a give and take situation. That was the case. What Fleetwood Mac "didn't need," Nicks said years later, was "another girl." It needed her "BDE," the bella donna energy she absorbed and tempered from the female rock icons who came before her: Janis Joplin and Grace Slick, yes, but also Bonnie O'Farrell of Delaney & Bonnie and Lydia Pense of Cold Blood.31 Their voices provided music a daring, gutsy, radio-unfriendly edge that the pop parade could not match. We've heard of Joplin and Slick, but not so much of O'Farrell (later Bramlett) and Pense. O'Farrell began her career as a blue-eyed blues backup vocalist, touring with the peripatetic who's who of southern US musicians (including Gregg Allman, Charlie Daniels, Stephen Stills, and Tina Turner). Her childhood was shattered by violence, so she fled to Los Angeles. In 1967, she met guitarist Delaney Bramlett during a bowling alley concert and married him. The duo released numerous albums of Nashville-style R&B, with the song "Soul Shake" standing out. Tours with Eric Clapton and George Harrison, who learnt slide guitar from Bramlett, followed. Mick Jagger invited O'Farrell to sing (or shrilly oversing) on "Gimme Shelter," but her husband despised the Stones and compelled her to decline the offer, claiming a sore throat. In a haze of drugs and highballs, the marriage ended. O'Farrell never stopped working, recording in blues, country, funk, and, most recently, gospel as a born-again Christian. Nicks met her through Olsen, who had hired Delaney & Bonnie drummer Jim Keltner for the Buckingham Nicks album released in 1973. Mick Fleetwood hired the Bramletts' daughter Bekka, a rockabilly artist, for his spin-off band the Zoo in the early 1990s. Bekka also subbed for Nicks on tour from 1993 to 1995 and replaced her as vocalist on Fleetwood Mac's Time (1995). Pense was born in San Francisco a year before Nicks. In the late 1960s, she sang brass-driven blues, and later, "East Bay grease" (funk). Blonde-haired, dark-eyed, and petite, she was arguably the mightiest of the powerful "blues belters" of the day, overwhelming the saxophones and brasses of her band Cold Blood and being positively likened to Janis Joplin's "Piece of My Heart." Pence's representative damaged her chances by signing her to two labels at the same time, which is illegal in the industry. Her career "stalled," and she was obliged to remain authentic and local—as "living proof that blazing talent is only one component of the formula for artistic success." For every Stevie Nicks, there are singers with limitless potential who, for a number of reasons—bad management, poor material, or awful airplay—can't seem to break through."

Nicks frequently acknowledged Joplin's influence, recalling a time in her early career, "a hot summer day in 1970," when her band Fritz opened for Joplin but played far too long. "Being yelled off the stage by Janis Joplin was one of the greatest honours of my life," she quipped before being inducted into the Rock and Roll Hall of Fame for the second time in 2019. Joplin scolded Fritz profanely, but Nicks waited after the rest of Fritz hurried away, enthralled by Joplin's voice and appearance. Although she did not include Patti Smith when discussing her musical upbringing, Amanda Petrusich made the following comparison: "Nicks is hyper feminine, intuitive, and bohemian; Smith is androgynous, cerebral, and gritty." "However, both are unusually astute chroniclers of their time and place."

Fleetwood Mac reinvented themselves as a blend of blues, rock, and folk, drawing inspiration from Nicks' writings and cassette tapes, as well as borrowings from the Beatles and Beach Boys. Three weeks after the El Carmen meeting, with Olsen behind the console in Sound City's Studio A, Fleetwood Mac began to do something it had never done before: produce a wide range of generically accessible music, including anodyne chill-outs (the single released in the United Kingdom, "Warm Ways"), good-time sing-alongs, a meditation on life's seasons, and an ode to a witch. John McVie had the most trouble adjusting to Fleetwood Mac's new reality, reportedly approaching Olsen and saying, "Keith, did you know we used to be a blues band?" "Yeah, I know, John," Olsen replied. "But it's a lot shorter to drive down to this bank."

Nicks contributed "Landslide," "Rhiannon," and a modified "Crystal" to "the white album," as Fleetwood Mac's 1975 record is called. She sang on every track. It's a collection of leftovers that is viewed as a successful "convergence" due, in part, to the arranging, embellishing, and polishing that got demos on the radio. The album was reportedly recorded in the first three months of 1975 with a July 11, 1975 release date, although the dates do not represent the material's lengthy gestation before Nicks and Buckingham joined Fleetwood Mac. Olsen bleached this material. Fleetwood Mac is the polar opposite of Motown, R&B, and Blaxploitation, suburbia rather than downtown, a treatment for the band's former blues that would not have succeeded if Nicks hadn't pushed so hard on tour. "We just played everywhere and sold that record," she told Uncut. "We kicked that album in the ass." The kicking began far before the record was even released. On May 5, 1975, the band began a two-leg, twelve-month tour with a concert in Edmonton, Alberta, followed by a mid-month show at the County Coliseum in El Paso, a jaunt through southern and central Texas, and a flight from Austin to Detroit for a swing through the Midwest and into the Northeast. "The great British-American-male-female-old-new-blues-rock-ballad band" toured for seven months on the first leg and nearly five months on the second leg (April 22 to September 5). Fleetwood Mac rushed to the Calgary Stampede and limped into the Trenton War Memorial, sandwiched between one-night appearances at fairgrounds, racetracks, colleges, and ice rinks. The band would leave for the next gig before the previous one's set concluded. It was a difficult relationship marred by a battle with Clifford Davis, a former Fleetwood Mac manager who, in one of the most audacious scam jobs in rock 'n' roll history, sent a less-skilled clone of the band on tour before the real one. Furthermore, Fleetwood Mac's gig in Vancouver on August 7, 1975, was disrupted by an aircraft engine failure (the band drove three hours from Seattle) and technical difficulties. "For two-thirds of the concert, [Nicks] could not be heard, and it seemed she would be relegated to just standing around looking beautiful." Buckingham's monitor detected her "strained" singing.

Nicks propelled the album to the top of the charts and into Rolling Stone, the music industry's leading newspaper, all while ruining her voice. She promoted Fleetwood Mac in locations as humble as Trod Nossel Studios in New Haven, Connecticut, where the owner gave away free tickets—the first fifty callers won!—to an up-close and personal Fleetwood Mac concert, which was also broadcast on local radio. She didn't respect her range and didn't get enough sleep, so her throat was constantly sore, she told her mother. But she worked tirelessly, and the crowd responded. "Lindsey brings a lyrically powerful guitar style and a strong sense of melody to the band." The Courier News of Blytheville, Arkansas, wrote that "Stevie's vocals are twangy, with an edge that provides a pleasant contrast to Christine's smoothness." Additional information was given to readers of the Capital Times in Madison, Wisconsin:

During a loud, foot-stomping song, she'll let loose with a rough, raspy, scratchy voice that says, "This mama knows what she's talking about."... But look at her: she's dressed in a delicate black dress with a gauzy black veil draped over her shoulders, and as drummer Mick Fleetwood produces a wall of strong rock behind her, she floats and glides around the stage as if listening to a minute. It appears weird at first, as if a glitter-obsessed adolescent singer devised a costume and image for herself and then wrapped the nearby band around her fantasies like a long black glove. Nicks' majorette razzle-dazzle, which included indigo denim bell-bottoms, an all-black top-hatted ensemble, chokers, silky cardigans, patterned skirts, and ankle- and knee-high boots, became the focal point of Fleetwood Mac performances, with "Rhiannon" serving as her musical highlight.

In 2020, Rolling Stone raved about a rendition on the television variety show Midnight Special on June 11, 1976, noting that after about four minutes, "there's a hush and you think the song is over." Instead, "the music picks up speed." [Nicks] looks through the camera into your soul. 'Take me as the wind, darling!' She's screaming now. 'Give me the sky!' Lindsey adds some powerful strums to the mix. Complete shawl and hair fusion. It's frightening how strongly Stevie quakes while repeating Rhiannon's name, and how steely she appears behind all that black lace. She literally jumps out of her boots for that nine-second final roar, and then she vanishes, just like Rhiannon." The earthy groove beneath the singing is a precise loop in the studio version: four tracks are dedicated to Buckingham's riff and strummed guitars, and the superimposed background vocals are impeccably enticing. Nicks elevates the song to new heights on Midnight Special, performing as Rhiannon directs and becoming "the coolest thing in the universe."

She presented herself to the public fearlessly and unapologetically, with the innate enthusiasm of a teenager developed and nurtured rather than suppressed in her twenties, thirties, and beyond. Nicks entered Rhiannon's universe and remained in a world of powers her bandmates had no idea about. She gradually demonstrated her abilities, first by transforming Fleetwood Mac into her own star vehicle, and then as a solo artist. Ballet motions and positions were incorporated into the myth, which she must have studied as a child (she later claimed to have taken classes with a Russian ballet teacher and built a dance studio in her Phoenix home). Despite bending her standing leg, photos show her being relatively flexible while stretching at the barre. In the tendu and sus-sous positions, her feet are slightly pointed. Despite flaws, her balletic onstage dances, combined with moves from other genres, distinguished her from other rock 'n' roll performers.

Christine McVie, in contrast to Nicks' "sinuous dancing and raw, gutsy vocal," sat behind a keyboard, flamboyant and stodgy, her dreams limited to sappy ballads about Harlequin romance-type love. The reviewers were drawn to their differences. They didn't appear to notice each other onstage, but their voices blended perfectly. They stayed together in between gigs, and it was McVie, not Nicks, who learned to put Buckingham in his place when his sassiness irritated

John McVie and Mick Fleetwood, the band's founding members. In the studio, Nicks deferred to Buckingham, but not on the road. The Welsh witch's power grew, and so did her reverence. Rumours debuted on February 4, 1977, before Egan's album. Fleetwood Mac released their eleventh album, but only their second with Nicks and Buckingham at the helm. The new Fleetwood Mac adhered to the three-minute, radio-friendly songwriting template, eliminating pretension and rambling improvisations that failed to chart. "By the time [Rumours] was made," eulogises journalist Jessica Hopper, "the personal liberties endowed by the social upheaval of the sixties had unspooled into unfettered hedonism." As such, it plays like a reaping: a highly polished post-hippie collapse, unaware that the free love era was coming to an end and there would be no turning back." Nicks' Rhiannon was in, but the mystical housewives from the 1960s sitcom Bewitched were out. "There was no knowledge of AIDS, Reagan had just left the governor's mansion, and people still thought of cocaine as non-addictive and strictly recreational," Hopper said. Rumours are a product of that era, and they serve as a standard against which we measure how good the 1970s were. After the test, Mick Fleetwood was harshly chastised in the press for becoming a fiendishly addicted alcoholic and leading his bandmates down the same path. Cocaine is derived from the pulp of the Erythroxylum coca bush leaves in the Andes Mountains, and it has been used in Incan spiritual ceremonies for millennia. Spanish colonists allowed enslaved Indigenous peoples to chew the leaves while they worked. When Pope Leo XIII, Queen Victoria, and Ulysses S. Grant fell down, they drank Vin Tonique Mariani (à la Coca du Pérou), a coca wine cocktail. Cocaine, refined by botanists and chemists, became an important medical ingredient and supplement in the 1890s. It soothed American newborns; salespeople sold it door to door alongside detergents and cosmetics; it improved soda fountains and, according to its supporters, helped with alcoholism. Coca-Cola is still available in red and white cans, the colours of the Peruvian flag, which previously supplied its happiness-making component. Southern politicians blamed African Americans' "sniffing" for increases in crime—"Negro Cocaine 'Fiends' Are a New Southern Menace," the New York Times blared—so the 1914 Harrison Act prohibited its sale for deeply racial reasons. Liquor prohibition followed. According to historian Robert Sabbag, cocaine became the drug of choice among musicians and film people in the 1920s and 1930s in search of lost time. [It] went virtually extinct after WWII, only to resurface during the rock era, when artists revived it." Cocaine evolved into the "life in the fast lane" narcotic. Superfly, a 1972 Blaxploitation film, compared it to "ambivalence" and "high fashion and sex versus addiction and crime." Traffickers from Medellin, Colombia, routed it through Los Angeles expat areas for distribution, annihilating the Westside's "drug princes,' ' whose supply came from Miami. Before the cartels took over and the atmosphere turned lethal, the "champagne drug" defined the celebrity high life and those who sought it. The fog and confusion rolled in, exposing the dealers and groupies who surrounded the pool as "leeches." The Eagles' 1976 single "Hotel California" describes the negative side as "desperation, panic, and imprisonment amid fountains of champagne, mediaeval gluttony, sexual deviants, and lines of cocaine on the mirror."

CHAPTER 3
COCAINE

Nicks formed a friendship with cocaine while filming Rumours. Everyone assumed it was far safer than heroin. She became addicted while working on Tusk and did not stop using the "Peruvian flake," as one of its nicknames was, until the Reagan era. She endangered her life and could become yet another tragic celebrity casualty. The premature deaths of addicted artists spawned the morbidly fetishistic "27 Club," a list of individuals who died at or near that age and then joined "the great gig in the sky." Nicks, like Fleetwood, has been open about her risk—"I was the worst drug addict"—and the time it took her to check out of the hotel. Clonazepam addiction followed cocaine addiction (she'll never forgive "Doctor Fuckhead" for hooking her on the anticonvulsant). She also "suffered long bouts of chronic fatigue syndrome" following an elective surgical procedure at the same time. Rumours topped the Billboard chart for thirty-one weeks before the tragedy, before the good old days turned bad. Rolling Stone ranked it number twenty-six on its "500 Greatest Albums of All Time" list in 2003, citing its symbolism: it spoke more to the crackup of the American psyche than to sleeping around. Rob Sheffield referred to it as "an album that has eerie soothing powers when you hear it in the midst of a crisis, which might be why it hits home right now, with our minute-by-minute deluge of apocalyptic news, the rottenest month to be an American since FDR died." "After all the tantrums and breakdowns and crying fits, the album ends with Stevie Nicks asking you point blank: 'Is it over now?'" 'Can you pick up the pieces and head home?' If the answers are 'no' and 'no,' play the album again."

The record's seamlessness and coherence are as surprising as its subject matter: complex stories about the band's inner lives, despite lineup changes and musical backgrounds. "Hey guys, why don't we chill out here and do some transcending and just write music about all this hassle?" Mick Fleetwood, who was dissolute, said this. The calmer tracks have a "desert hearts" vibe to them between the fuck you of "Go Your Own Way," and the issues of divorce and abjection have an odd precedent in the testicular fantasy of screwing whomever lover comes your way in a cornfield. The front cover, a dream image turned into best-selling memorabilia, shows Nicks spinning in black while Rhiannon and Fleetwood are dressed in Renaissance Faire garb—the patriarch with a foot on a stool and a pair of wooden balls hanging from his belt (good-luck charms he claimed he stole from a toilet in a bar). She raises and bends her left leg on top of his, while he holds a crystal (recycled from the previous Fleetwood Mac album) into which she appears to stare. Outtakes, or photos that did not make the cover, are more informal, even playful. According to Nigel Williamson of Uncut magazine, Fleetwood Mac were "rock's greatest living soap opera," but they were also a group of musicians who had a contractual obligation to arrive at the studio at two p.m. for a twelve-hour music-making shift. The album's title was inspired by gossip, proto-Melrose Place sordidness, Bacchic revelries, and nostalgie de la boue, and it also serves as a convenient explanation of the lyrical and musical content. These don't add up: Nicks and Buckingham fought while recording "You Make Loving Fun"—and "I don't want to live with you, either!"—but delivered a gloriously euphoric chorus. Christine McVie sings in her silky alto voice on "Songbird," "I love you like never before," which could be a reference to a hypothetical romance or her growing love for John despite their failed marriage. The novel Fear of Flying and the film An Unmarried Woman place the album in popular culture. Hippies evolved into swingers who threw important parties. Rumours date back to the mature 1960s, as well as the 1970s. It confronts the implications of free love and looks into a void of pleasure pursued solely for the sake of enjoyment.

Nicks had evolved. Buckingham taxed her, and rumours did too. "She loved to laugh," recalls Ken Caillat. "She was so wonderful back then, so down to earth." "What a transformation she would go through." The same could be said about the era represented by Rumours—its good, bad, and neglected aspects. Her lyrics from the album's creation and the long, long tour that followed document the transformation: "The 24th of August, 1977." On the plane once more. Lindsey is his usual arrogant self. I am gradually realising that Lindsey and I are coming to an end. "It's so satisfying to see good love turn bad." "Seattle," he replies later. Christine is causing me concern. I'm hoping to get some spiritual advice from somewhere. "Where have my crystal visions gone when I need them?" "I'm writing songs as well as prose," he says later. 'Gather the curtains, gather the darkness, gather me if only for a moment, gather the seconds because they may vanish soon, gather the blessings because the years are showing.' "

Fleetwood Mac fans prefer the grittier opening and closing tracks on Rumours side B over the pop of side A. "The Chain" combines elements from demo songs created by all of the musicians. The song begins with a modal Dobro resonator guitar, a sluggish kick drum, and murky, stormy lyrics. The opening guitar riff is a reworking of "Lola (My Love)," a 1973 Buckingham Nicks song that was particularly popular during the duo's Alabama tour. The words for "The Chain" arrived at the end, thanks to Nicks' inspired pen, preventing the collection of outtakes from becoming an outtake itself. The three vocalists' close harmony on "listen to the wind blow" is mysterious because of Nicks' alter ego as "Rhiannon." The mood is heavy, and the pacing is masterful, culminating in the album's most memorable musical moment: a quick crash cymbal that is abruptly muted on the upbeat of the measure's second beat, effectively ending the first chorus. It's the same as sneering or spitting things out in disgust. Throughout, the ensemble sings together, musically contrasting their contentious personal issues. The line "Chain, keep us together" seems to be a request. The coda gives a taste of what a Fleetwood Mac live improvisation sounds like, as the song's gritted-teeth tension is released. John McVie's transitional ten-note bass riff (derived from Christine McVie's abandoned song "Keep Me There") is likely the album's most memorable moment. The ending's synchronised vocals imply, incorrectly, adamantine resolve.

"Gold Dust Woman," the final track on side B, imagines California as both the Wild West and an eastern Shangri-La. The final track is raw and primal, in stark contrast to the polished sensuality of the previous tracks. "The definitive magical Stevie Nicks vocal would have to be 'Gold Dust Woman,'" Caillat says, laughing. "She was possibly possessed at the end of that song." He also stated that he is unable to listen to the record despite devoting "at least 3,000 hours" to it. "I spent everything on that, you know, there's nothing left of me... and I just wish I could enjoy it like everyone else." However, every time I hear it, I recall every detail, every conflict, every battle. As a result, it's not as enjoyable for me. The end of "Gold Dust Woman" did not require the same level of dedication from the murdered producer. The jamboree was unplanned. In a 1976 interview, Nicks described "Gold Dust Woman" in terms most high-school girls could understand. "It's about groupie-type ladies," she confided in me, "about women who stand around and give me and Christine dirty looks but as soon as a guy comes in the room they are overcome with smiles." She has also stated that it is about success, which reveals some of the secret to her success: a combination of "rock" singing, which is associated with men, and full-bodied whispering huskiness, which breaks into a thin high register, which is associated with women. Then there's the price-of-success reading, which transforms the song into a "black widow" of cocaine, resulting in increased sensitivity to touch, hearing, and sight, as well as anger and paranoia. Buckingham's primary guitar line incorporates unusual sitar-like effects and bays at the moon. Fleetwood shatters the glass with a cowbell.

In a book about gender and rock, Mary Kearney provides both micro and macro perspectives on the song, describing it as a "tale of a heartless, drug-addicted woman who preys on a man's affections only to leave him broken and disheartened" and an example of a "demeaning" representation of a female by a female songwriter. According to Kearney, the majority of such portrayals come from men, about whom Nicks seldom sings on her own. Still, the majority of "Gold Dust Woman" covers, fifty and counting, are by women, and both the original and the variations capture Nicks' rueful passion.

Christine McVie's warm, reverberant "Songbird" provides the atmosphere that the rest of the album lacks. "One of the defining aspects of Rumours is claustrophobia," Tim Sommer stated. That is, "sonic claustrophobia," in which the listener feels trapped within Fleetwood's tightly closed hi-hat. To enhance the sense of liberation and openness, "Songbird" was recorded at UC Berkeley's Zellerbach Hall rather than Sausalito's Power Plant. Caillat chose the venue because he had been captivated by the song since first hearing her perform it and wanted to give it a unique feel. "As a surprise for Christine, I had asked that a bouquet of roses be placed on her piano, illuminated from above by three coloured spotlights."I was determined to set the tone! . . . We dimmed the house lights so Christine could only see the flowers and the piano, with the spotlight shining down from above. She was about to cry. Then she started to play. The piano dominates the recording, with only a subtle acoustic guitar accompaniment.

As "The Chain" demonstrates, the harmonies on the album are tight and close, as the Power Plant's acoustics require. The electric guitars and keyboards share the wah pedals, while the acoustic guitar lines are equalised to pick up higher frequencies. The glossiness is similar to, but not the same as, Brian Wilson's aural watercolours. The album is based on the placement of distinct sounds across bridges and between verses and choruses, so the layers of overdubs are large enough for the ear to isolate each line. Christine McVie's "Don't Stop" is perhaps the best example of one voice part being grafted onto another, but it's also the album's bluntest, least nuanced song, so perfectly calibrated for the baby-boomer hit parade that it became fodder for Bill Clinton's 1992 presidential campaign. McVie had tossed it around before the Rumours recordings, and it, contrary to the lyrics, is from the jungle piano era. McVie and Buckingham collaborate, singing in unison in the verses and finishing each other's phrases in the chorus, blending her voice with his. Each seems to have forgotten what the other did. Nicks is barely audible, while the other two members of the band grind along, pausing at the base of the crescendos and restarting to fill them out. "Yesterday's Gone" was going to be the album title. Rumours (spelled in English as a nod to the band's past) won out.

Nicks played the tambourine and other instruments during the early track sessions, but she was not mic'd, and the band would later re-record all of her percussion contributions. Her voice defined this Fleetwood Mac incarnation, but because she did not contribute any instrumental recordings, she was often left with nothing to do for hours at a time. The original Sausalito Power Plant featured two studios, a Jacuzzi, a basketball court, a speedboat, and a restaurant with its own chef. One of the walls in Studio A was decorated with a sunburst pattern, while the other was covered in colourful giant petals. Sly Stone, a producer and artist, designed and furnished an underground lair with a large red lip entrance and synthetic red fur walls. Nicks sat on the four-poster bed, writing in her notebook, practising macramé, and playing the piano (which Stone had connected to a console, allowing him to record while prone).

She wrote a number-one song, "Dreams," in this semi-sleazy setting, setting the melody and lyrics atop three chords. She brought it to Studio B and recorded "a rough take, just me singing solo and playing piano." Buckingham was angry at the time, according to Nicks, but he listened with a smile. "What was going on between us was sad—we were couples who couldn't make it through," Nicks stated at the time. "But, as musicians, we still respected each other." When the original rising harmonic pattern (Fmaj7, G, A minor) was expanded into an introduction and three-part form, that smile revealed the song's potential. The first line is followed by a pre-chorus and a declaration of regret—"what you lost / what you had"—which is made more painful by adding a ninth to the F chord and a seventh to the G chord. It is followed by the "thunder" chorus, the second verse, the pre-chorus again, and two more chorus repetitions. It registers different moods, warm and cool, similar to a musical mood ring.

Caillat admits in his account of arranging and recording that the demo is more moody than the finished product. Nicks' vocal breaks suggest feelings influencing cognition, while the pitch-worrying reveals a folk influence that the studio removed. The tune is based on only five such pitches and does not like to end in time with its accompaniment. D must commit to C but hesitates, giving the song its "hypnotic" quality. The hypnosis intensified in the studio, becoming more akin to the trance described in the text as a result of sound looping, particularly the bass drum and hi-hat sound at the beginning. Caillat describes how he played through the cassette tape in search of the "most perfect" sample:

We couldn't find eight perfect bars, so Mick had to play nearly a minute of the verse to ensure they were completely steady. It took approximately sixteen seconds to play eight bars. At fifteen inches per second, this required cutting approximately twenty feet of tape from the drum take and splicing it together, front to back, to create a continuous loop. Our tape loop would be a twenty-foot-wide circle...

She sang the song eight or nine times, but something was off. She couldn't get back into the mood she was in when she first sang it. But she was a fighter who wouldn't give up. Lindsey accompanied her singing with an acoustic guitar. Nope. She tried to smoke a joint. Better. The big guns arrived—Courvoisier. Interesting. She experimented with a magic bump [a small spoonful of white stuff]. Nothing compared to her original voice.

Eventually, some of the original vocals were recovered and saved, as were the Sly Stone-inspired reveries. In his album review, John Rockwell rejected the "trippy" lyrics, but praised Nicks' "husky, nasal, sensuously confident soprano" and flower child image as a complement to Christine's fuss-free alto "earthiness."

Nicks frequently gives her "kids" (songs) enigmatic, one-word titles. "Dreams" is the first of several. The opening guitar swells establish the mood (similar to the Mellotron in the Beatles' "Strawberry Fields Forever"), and the phrase "thunder" is accompanied by a cymbal crash. The line "Now here you go again / You say you want your freedom" is intended for Lindsey Buckingham, but it also expresses a universal emotion for anyone going through a breakup. After much deliberation, "Dreams" was inserted between Buckingham's "Second Hand News" and "Never Going Back Again," so that his harsh goodbyes frame her "you'll regret this." "You can go your own way / You can roll like thunder, yeah yeah," he sings in an early take of "Go Your Own Way," whereas the final version includes the line "You can call it another lonely day." She took away his thunder.

"Dreams" contains silky R&B textures as well as the moodiness of Steely Dan's Aja, which was released the same year as Rumours. Caillat wrapped a rubber band around a windscreen and placed it on the microphone, making sure the windscreen was about a half-inch from the front of the mic, to increase the song's intimacy, or "proximity." 'Keep your lips up against that windscreen,' I'd say, and I'd have a lot of bottom, to which I could add top if I wanted." He used a swell pedal and a revolving (Leslie) speaker to smooth out the rough edges of the assault on the guitar. The bass throbs in a syncopated two-note pattern when the bass-drum pedal is pressed. The background singing reminds Caillat of the Beach Boys, while the phaser on the hi-hat creates a "slightly squishy and swirling" sound reminiscent of the theremin-infused megahit "Good Vibrations." The vibraphone in the Spinners' song "I'll Be Around" may have inspired Caillat to use the instrument's crystal-clear tone in the second pre-chorus. Using a Wurlitzer in the verse-chorus transition and a Fender Rhodes in the chorus gave the song the "classy" sound Caillat desired (by the twenty-fourth take). However, "Dreams" remained Nicks' tune. She is, in her own words, "on the mic, bringing both the thunder and the rain, her unguarded, open-veined rasp painting every one of her crystal visions in such rich, vibrant colour that they actually sound like they're causing Buckingham's guitars to openly weep."

Despite the band's misery, this song, like the others on Rumours, demonstrates that bad lovers can create excellent music. Nicks discusses Buckingham's possessions and losses, advising him to "listen carefully to the sound of... loneliness." Nicks warns her evil lover, both here and in the magnificent, abandoned "Silver Springs," that her words will always echo in his mind. He can't escape it, and Buckingham never has. The concept of haunting, as a fusion of the present and the past, persists.

The story of the song's creation and abandonment reflects Nicks' precarious second-tier status in Fleetwood Mac at the time; it also foreshadows her first departure from the band. Nicks most likely had it during the first leg of Fleetwood Mac's 1975-76 tour, when her relationship with Buckingham was on the rocks. The band would have passed through Silver Springs, Maryland, on their way to a performance in Washington, DC. She chose the town's name for the song and recorded a rough draft. "You'll never get away from the sound of the woman who loved you," she says, despite his lack of confidence in her. Buckingham despised it but saw its potential, including the possibility of removing the stabbing lyrics. He and Caillat began planning it.

Sections are similar to Peter Green's "Albatross," a Fleetwood Mac single released in 1968. "Silver Springs" also includes country intonations that may recall Nicks' grandfather, Aaron Jess Nicks Sr. The chorus descends into A minor before reaching a spellbinding, then shattering, climax in a shimmering translucent C/F major heard high on the keyboard. The sylph transforms into the sorceress in the words and melody, exacting revenge on her former suitor. She might just rip his heart out, as he did hers. The drama is played out in a number of Nicks' power ballads, the most powerful of which is this one, thanks to the gradual co-opting of the listener's attention and the upward push of the chorus, an act of sheer will that returns minor to major. The mood shifts from deceptive serenity (keyboard) to resignation (Nicks' iterated "I don't want to know"), followed by the chorus' click track-aided breakthrough and the provocation of Buckingham's solo, which elicits Nicks' rage in the end. "Was I just a fool?" The question has never been answered, and it has never been asked.

The song progresses from a halcyon lethargy and relatively bland effect to a cri de coeur that pushes the song's pitches away, as does Buckingham's cheerful confidence. Nicks rises above the mat at the lowest point, as evidenced by the alignment and assembly of the tracks into booming unison statements. (In the chorus, the melodic line rises, but the harmony falls, with first-inversion A minor giving way to first-inversion G and F major.) Caillat remembers practising plane crashes in the studio.

We began by recording "Silver Springs" on Wednesday using the Fender Rhodes keyboard, electric guitar, bass, and drums, as well as Stevie's vocals. We needed to perfect the basic track; eventually, we'd add a grand piano, but for the time being, the Rhodes would suffice. Laying out a song in this manner frequently required us to rely on our imaginations to fill in the gaps until the other sections were added.

We obtained approximately nineteen takes, some of which were complete and others were only partials. But none of them were correct, and we soon ran out of steam. Perhaps relying on our imaginations wasn't sufficient. To break up the work, Richard [Dashut] and Mick did a few quick sketches. As strange as it may sound, reenacting a plane crash was one of their favourite activities. It happened in Sausalito. Caillat and the band listened to the work they had done in Los Angeles and decided that the song needed much more work; it still sounded "thin" and "empty" and had to be cut.

According to Rolling Stone, in a 1991 BBC radio interview, Nicks stated that Fleetwood, the band's manager, met with her in the Record Plant parking lot to inform her that "Silver Springs" had been cut due to its length. He claimed that the maximum length of an LP side before sound quality degraded was 22 minutes. "Second Hand News" could have been cut to make room for "Silver Springs" on Rumours, but no. "A lot of [other] reasons" existed for cutting it. Buckingham's difficulty getting past the lyrics was one of them, as was the importance of equal representation for the other songwriters on the album. "Silver Springs" would have been Nicks' third ballad, after "Dreams" and "Gold Dust Woman." Caillat wanted to keep the song and continue working on it in Los Angeles, but Nicks was devastated. She walked out of the parking lot after launching a derogatory tirade against Fleetwood. He wondered if she'd return. "When I first recorded 'Silver Springs,' I gave it to my mother as a present," Nicks said, exacerbating her anger and embarrassment. "My mother would never take a penny from me"—in fact, given her husband's success in business, she didn't need to—"so I figured the only way I could actually give her some money was to give her a song to save for a rainy day." She received everything—publishing, royalties, etc... She had even opened an antique shop called Silver Spring Emporium. Then they took it off the record, resulting in a flop gift. 'Well, guess what, Mom?' it asked. It is not going on record, and I apologise."

'Silver Springs' ended up on the B-side of the single 'Go Your Own Way' as well as greatest-hits compilations. The pain persisted, and the band and Warner Brothers capitalised on it in the emotional performance that served as the official music video. Buckingham's eyes flash across the stage as Nicks sings the line. "Really, I don't wanna know," which differs from the original "Baby, I don't wanna know." "But you won't forget me," she says. The rest of the 1997 performance is a staring match, expertly recorded, with the two of them making room on stage for each other. The first verses' pleas are rejected as the sound rises to astonishing emotional intensity before artificially fading. "When we're [onstage] there singing songs to each other, we probably say more to each other than we ever would in real life," Nicks said. She detested "Go Your Own Way" as much as he despised "Silver Springs," especially the third verse. "Every time those words ['packin' up, shackin' up is all you want to do'] would come on stage," she went on to say, "I wanted to go over and kill him." He was aware of this. He certainly pushed my buttons with that. She seemed to be saying, 'I'll make you suffer for leaving me,' which I did. Other renditions of "Silver Springs" replicate the standoff; it became an obsession for the two of them, a publicly repeated what-could-have-been catharsis. During a 2004 event in Madison, Wisconsin, Nicks walks away from her microphone with the back of her palm over her mouth in what appears to be an emotional moment, but then immediately begins dancing, spinning, and air drumming, facing Fleetwood and with her back to the audience. She then picks up her microphone stand and spins it to face Buckingham while they perform another set-to. The version released on Nicks' 2001 solo album Crystal Visions features rerecorded guitar lines, delays, swells, and harmony.This version has a much faster, harder pace and fades out on the chorus rather than returning defeated to the beginning.

The song "I Don't Want to Know" by Nicks replaced "Silver Springs" on Rumours. It has an I-V-IV-V chord sequence, handclaps, and a bright McCartney-style bass line that bounces from one chord's root to another, reminiscent of Buckingham Nicks and an earlier popular-music syntax. Another throwback on the album is "Never Going Back Again," which highlights Buckingham's picking style. Caillat instructed him to change his strings every twenty minutes while tracking the tune. "I wanted to get the best sound on every one of his picking parts," he said. "I'm sure the roadies wanted to kill me." Restringing the instrument three times an hour was inconvenient. But Lindsey had several parts in the song, and each one sounded fantastic." The song's style is rustic, reminiscent of late 1960s San Francisco folk culture. Hearing "I Don't Want to Know" and "Never Going Back Again" alongside "Dreams" reveals changes in popular music over the decade. Keyboards and a heavy bass sound over crisp beats are the gin of blue-eyed soul and the tonic of seventies light rock, with maracas, tambourine, and vibraphone added for good measure. The original Fleetwood Mac and the Southern California recording industry appropriated African American music. Songs took time to discover their identities. According to a track sheet from August 21, 1976, "Dreams" was originally titled "Spinners." The groove made me think of the R&B group of the same name, particularly the song "I'll Be Around."

Buckingham expanded his role in Rumours halfway through the year-long production process. In May 1976, the remaining members of the band and the project parted ways. Buckingham returned to work before the others, reworking a number of the songs in Los Angeles. Stephen Davis recalls the final stages of recording and how his time in Sausalito nearly went to waste: March, 1976. After three agonising months, Fleetwood Mac was leaving the Record Plant and returning to their homes in Los Angeles to finish the new album. They played their tapes, which did not sound right in a different studio. There was panic until someone discovered Producer's Workshop, a mixing room tucked away among the shady porn theatres on Hollywood Boulevard, and their tapes sounded good enough to work with. While Stevie and her friends went on vacation in Acapulco, Lindsey and the two producers scrapped almost everything they'd done so far except the drum tracks, and Fleetwood Mac began dubbing in new instrumental parts and all of the vocals. The subsonic vibrations of the group's pain filled the air again as the three writers—Stevie, Chris, and Lindsey—continued to telegraph punches through their new songs. Carol Ann Harris, the studio's attractive, young receptionist, worked there. She was in her mid-20s, smart and blond, with blue eyes and a lovely grin. Lindsey started dating her, and she began hanging out at the studio after work to be with him. Harris was Buckingham's on-again, off-again lover between Rumours and his second solo album, Go Insane, in 1984. Her naive visions of the rock 'n' roll high life collided with the nightmare of physical abuse, which she avenges in her memoir.

Buckingham's hands squeezing her neck, his eyes bulging with rage; Mick Fleetwood's dismissal as manager; burglaries; an eviction; a car accident; and the "cutthroat competitive battle" with Nicks that turned into a "all-out-war" after Nicks' first solo album's success. Concerning the "subsonic vibrations of the group heartache," Fleetwood Mac benefited from, then became enslaved to, its own melodrama. The musicians' love-hate songs from their twenties and thirties have never truly left them.

The tape problem began in Sausalito, when the Record Plant's twenty-four-track system proved insufficient for the intricate vocal and instrumental texture envisioned for Fleetwood Mac II. More groups of sounds were "bounced—mixed down to a single track—to save space," and "over 60 tracks" were printed on a "single [master] reel of tape," according to specialists Richard Buskin of webzine Sound on Sound. Another stumbling block was the lifeless acoustics of the cushioned, smoke-filled studios and control room, as well as the thin, dull sound that travelled through the lines. Caillat and Dashut turned knobs and adjusted feeds in a desperate attempt to improve the sound. The deck's wear and tear, as well as the leaching of oxide from the frequently rewound multitrack tape, harmed the sound even more. The percussion's high frequencies were especially impacted.

After two months in Sausalito, the band returned to Los Angeles, with some songs unfinished or, in the case of "Silver Springs," requiring cuts. Caillat and Dashut returned to their regular workplace, Wally Heider Recording on Sunset and Cahuenga Boulevard, hoping to save the Rumours master tape, which was sounding increasingly bad. The solution was discovered in another studio on Beverly Boulevard, ABC Dunhill, by a technician named Bob Bullock, who developed a system for transferring tracks between the second-generation backup, or "safety" master, and the original first-generation master. Bullock went back to the drums' original multitrack and tried to mix it with the current master (the one with all the tracks) to bring the drums back to life. He had to manually account for the varying speeds of different tape machines, which was mind-boggling. He also had to go through the bounce history to locate the higher-quality original recordings. "When it came time to mix Rumours (five months later), we found a pristine little mix room that specialised in super clean electronics called Producers Workshop (where Lindsey met Carol)," Caillat goes on to explain. Dashut and I worked on the final version of Rumours for two weeks over Christmas in 1976."

Meanwhile, Buckingham experimented with the guitar sections of his most popular songs, as well as the percussion on "Secondhand News." The background music is a simple shuffle with locomotive strumming.

As if in response to Buckingham's singing, a bright acoustic guitar (in Nashville tuning) decorates the end of each verse phrase, and a distorted second electric guitar injects energy halfway through before bursting into an affirmative lead part in the coda and fade-out. Buckingham objected to Fleetwood's drum pattern after hearing the initial mix, and when the rest of the band went on hiatus in May 1976, he recorded an additional percussion part, presumably inspired by the Bee Gees' "Jive Talkin'"—the sixteenth-note popping sound—played on the back of an office chair. The tapping contributes to the hook of a song that is essentially all hook, with syncopated "bow ba dow" scatting and the chorus's eponymous line repeated over and over, as well as Buckingham's "Lay me down in the tall grass and let me do my stuff."

The band remained together despite Buckingham's declaration to the contrary in "Go Your Own Way," whose lyrics are unrelated to the music's hook and thrust. The song is deeper than it appears at first, thanks to the use of a doubling six-string acoustic guitar at the end of phrases to provide a counter rhythm to the electric guitar's straight-ahead chugging. Fleetwood, a normally quiet drummer, employs subtle tom-tom interjections in the verses before unleashing a thudding bass drum on the "four on the floor" chorus. Buckingham planned for unpredictability in Fleetwood's section before the first chorus, and Fleetwood attempted to accommodate it. ("Street Fighting Man," by the Rolling Stones, was most likely an inspiration.) The drums take their own path before locking in on the lyrics "go your own way," which Fleetwood attributes to incompetence and dyslexia. In the chorus, decorum and restraint are dropped, and spitefulness emerges. Caillat claims Fleetwood became "distracted" while playing the hi-hat and instead kept time with the kick drum. The drumming in the song's outro is extremely quiet. Fleetwood avoids cymbal smashes and long fills. Christine McVie sings earnestly and hilariously (given the circumstances) about making "Lovin' Fun," beginning with a Fender Rhodes keyboard and Clavinet (one of Sly Stone's). The verses alternate between g-minor (vi) and F-major (V) chords before transitioning to the Bb tonic in the chorus (the key relationship may be reversed depending on the listener's perception). The chimes that respond to "ways of magic" in the chorus are a pop-rock cliché, but the lush background voices and stuttering drumming in the chorus are more inventive, despite the Byrds' overall influence. The heavenly tune is contrasted with the power ballad "Oh Daddy," which is about a failing marriage (if not love). John McVie's melodic bass interacts with his soon-to-be ex-wife's Hammond organ playing, adding authenticity to the sad sound—how humiliating for him to play on a song about his late lover's sensual desires. The rock 'n' roll urban outlaw song features powerful emphases in the piano's lower range and gentler guitar beats over a sharp snare. Bruce Springsteen's "Lost in the Flood" is one example, as is Bon Jovi's "Wanted Dead or Alive." The castanet flourish on the bridge ensures that the illusion is understood. Buckingham incorporates harmonics into his strumming, which is mic'd and equalised to emphasise the metallic tone of the strings while filling out the higher range.

The line between love and hate is thin, and it is crossed frequently on the album, as well as in the marketing of the amours impropre and the globe ninety-six-stop tour, which ran from February 24, 1977, to August 30, 1978. Legions of people saw the band perform live in ten- to fifteen-thousand-seat venues, and even more purchased the original vinyl edition of Rumours or listened to the singles on repeat. Nicks bid farewell to the days of station wagons and motels, but she brought her childhood friend Robin Snyder along for company and occasional dog sitting. Fleetwood Mac travelled by private jet and stayed in five-star hotels and presidential suites painted pink and outfitted with white grand pianos, leading a life of debauched decadence complete with personal caterers, masseuses, and security guards, swilling fine wine, ingesting cocaine from Heineken caps, and giving inarticulate interviews. Travel breaks provided opportunities for wild antics, such as Nicks' martial arts photo shoot with a large red-haired Australian bodyguard named Bob Jones.

The UK shows felt like a homecoming for Fleetwood and the McVies, while the Southeast US dates attracted Buckingham Nicks fans. Girls from all over the country arrived dressed as Nicks, having waited all night in line for tickets. Critics praised the ninety-minute set for its overall excellence and the entertaining Nicks-McVie dynamic. John Rockwell attributed the women's "highflying harmonies" to a Mamas & Papas imprint reminiscent of Changing Times, emphasising the band's "illusion" of a "supportive community." In his opinion, Nicks was both a siren and an angel, with her "sexy, mysterious ballads" including "seraphic posturing." Her demeanour was "compelling and endearing," but also "a little stagey" (which is not uncommon for stage performances). "We're not God's gifts as technicians," Fleetwood said when asked about his skill set by Rockwell. "We make more mistakes than some bands," admitted Nicks. "But there is a very loving thing up there, and it comes across." Her voice broke once more as she expressed her love. Sleep deprivation, self-medication, and arduous travel all had an impact on Nicks' intonation; in some of the footage, she is noticeably out of tune, and the Syracuse event had to be cancelled to give her throat time to recover. A speech therapist encouraged her to sing in a higher range. Fleetwood was aware that the band's music would have to change, but he appeared unconcerned about the situation. His group was unconcerned with genealogy or consistent influence.

Following Buckingham's wisdom tooth extraction, the band performed at Long Island's Nassau Coliseum. Nicks compensated for his onstage sluggishness by stretching her voice even more and providing material for horrifying newspaper comments about her "shaggy-haired love object... mystique," "drunken sailor" gracelessness, and "valiant" but failed effort to reach the appropriate notes.Thus, Peter Herbst, the perpetrator of these insults, said goodbye to his backstage pass.

Nicks dismissed the criticisms in favour of her own perspective on the lengthy, exhausting tour: she and the other musicians "basically" enjoyed each other. Onstage, "the problems, fights, arguments, and disagreements" disappeared. Nobody wanted to give up. Touring was profitable and generally enjoyable. When it wasn't, "it was just, grit your teeth and bear it."

Buckingham clenched his teeth and spit. "By the time we conclude this tour," he told a backstage camera crew, "we will have done 98 gigs since the end of March, or when was it? End of February/beginning of March. I've played 98 shows and am tired of it! Finished!" He said, "I hate it, I hate it."

Tusk, the follow-up to Rumours, bid farewell to the 1970s by completely reworking everything Fleetwood Mac had done since the two Californians met—Christine McVie's "Warm Ways" and "Over My Head," as well as all the major-key tracks on Rumours and the "white album." Stagflation set in, and the relaxed attitude dissipated. Buckingham, Fleetwood Mac's artistic director, detected the shift in the zeitgeist and responded to it, albeit idiosyncratically, with the general agreement of his colleagues. Following the conclusion of the Rumours tour, he lavished on a double album, which enraged Warner Brothers management while delighting cult fans. Buckingham started Tusk from scratch, free of the pressure to create an overtly commercial sequel to Rumours, experimenting at home and at Village Studios (housed in a former Masonic temple on the outskirts of Santa Monica) for months on end with bits and pieces of material that refused to coalesce. Lore depicts him screaming himself hoarse while lying on the floor and setting up a four-track recorder in a bathroom; there is footage of him singing into a microphone taped to the resonant brown tiles in a push-up position.

Tusk's 15th track, "I Know I'm Not Wrong," does away with its own hook, a small cadential pattern played on accordion by Christine McVie that is then covered by a guitar solo. The previous track, the bluesy "Brown Eyes," is sha-la-la apotheosis. The title track demonstrates a primitivist preference for tom-toms over synthesisers. The University of Southern California's Spirit of Troy marching band enters Dodger Stadium, and someone moans, "We are savage-like," as brasses cascade and batons spin. The beer-soaked arrangement and recording session occurred on Monday afternoon, June 4, 1979, while the Dodgers were away. The album's master tapes include random cymbal crashes, guitars tuned down to the bass range, and the thumping of a tissue box and slabs of flesh, but the total production cost for such strange, cheap effects was significantly more than $1 million. "One of the reasons Tusk cost so much is that we happened to be at a studio that was charging a fuck of a lot of money," Buckingham explained in a statement. We were in the studio for about ten months working on Tusk, and we ended up with twenty songs. Rumours took the same amount of time to spread. We saved money because we were in a lower-cost studio. There's no denying the cost, but I think it was taken out of context."

Nonsense. The band members tailored Village Studio D to their preferences. Tina Morris, the current manager, gave me a tour of the facility, which is a maze of interconnected recording spaces for large and small ensembles. On the wall facing the parking lot, a sun-blasted artwork titled Isle of California (1972) depicts a torn-up Arizona-California border following the "big one," the mega-earthquake predicted to devastate the West Coast. Nicks designed a bathroom with blue, bronze, and Indian mosaic tiles for her private use in Studio D, the large space in the centre of the first floor—a popular spot, Morris told me, when the facility hosts parties. I asked Nicks about his preferred dynamic microphone, a Sennheiser 441, and if Buckingham and Nicks still consider the studio to be a home. They do, and modern superstars continue to reserve Studio D and the more modern B for extended periods of time. (The Red Hot Chili Peppers were playing when I arrived.) Mick Fleetwood, the band's ostensible manager, sat on an overstuffed chair in the lounge, which led to the console room and the live area beyond. The chair remains next to the band's black leather sofa. Buckingham panelled a side room with imported quartersawn zebrawood to create the darker, deeper acoustic he envisioned for the record. The band's exotic tchotchkes—the voodoo items hung on the walls for the Tusk sessions—stay, but the lamps, mirrors, live-room rugs, and equipment don't. Before getting down to business, the wealthy celebrities ate, drank, and breathed. The footage from the recording sessions (most likely shot by Richard Dashut, the album's second producer) shows how young they were in 1978. All expenses included the cost of furniture, panelling, and plumbing, as well as the cost of recording and undoing take after take of the twenty songs on Tusk. The two albums, with their lavish inner and outer covers (the purposefully unappealing cover depicts Ken Caillat's dog Scooter attacking his leg), were released in 1979 for $15.98 before falling off the charts and into bargain bins. Tusk sold four million copies in its first year, going quadruple platinum in the final days of the album, but given the label's expectations and Rumours' much greater success, it appeared to be a flop. Tusk's sales were severely hampered by the Westwood One radio network, which broadcast the entire album on its release date, October 12, 1979, allowing fans to record it for free. The record is now regarded as both Fleetwood Mac's deconstruction and easy listening. Sam Anderson's review of the album is clear and compelling, and it includes a sarcastic ode to the consumable sounds of the 1970s, as well as the fictions that the FM dial freely promoted. Tusk represents a referendum on the persuasive power of sha-la-la. "The Crystal Palace of Soft Rock will not save anyone," he says, referring to Rumours and Eagles albums like The Long Run.

It's a lovely but frail structure, incapable of protecting us from even the most minor of life's assaults, let alone the more serious mud clods, cannonballs, and stinger missiles that accompany marriage, parenthood, ageing, and death. Soft Rock's Crystal Palace will crumble. It has no purpose. Do not put your trust in it. Tusk is an excellent album because of how quickly and mercilessly it exposes this falsehood. It's more than just a late 1970s pop relic; it's a work of art that continues to speak to sentient beings today.

Anderson bases his claim on the first and second tracks, "Over & Over" and "The Ledge," which he describes as a thesis and antithesis of a mauve-and-orange Malibu sunset and a harsh fluorescent bulb waking. On the former, everything is in its proper place; there is no out-of-tune pitch, wrinkled cloth, or dent in the contour. But, before you know it, the essential oils have clouded your judgement and the album has moved into the 1980s. "The Ledge" is classic grunge: part skiffle, half punk, with a lick or two lifted from the Beatles' "Wild Honey Pie." Buckingham recorded "The Ledge" at home with a drum machine, speeding up his voice to sound like Nicks in the background. The lyrics are nursery rhymes with a cruel twist ("counting on my fingers, counting on my toes"). The phrase "slipping through your fingers" has been shortened to "flipping you the finger."" Consider that the album's title is Fleetwood Mac slang meaning "dick." Buckingham tells us to screw ourselves by looking over the ledge at the broken relationships below.

"The defining tension of Tusk is perfection versus destruction, gloss versus mess—the lure of soft rock versus the barb of art rock," Anderson goes on to explain. It is the place where intense artistic control yields to raggedness, where chaos and order dance in a cloud of whirling scarves. The album definitely has five songs too many, and a few tracks are two minutes too long, but that's the price of genius: excess, bombast, arrogance, and getting carried away." Peter Green, the founder of Fleetwood Mac, expanded the twelve-bar, three chord blues format by looking for tones in music that he had "experienced" through mescaline and LSD ingestion, and Buckingham added to the enrichment.

Tusk toggles like this, and the dials in Village Studio D turn 180 degrees between songs. It's brilliant because it anticipates its own failure. Buckingham has always received credit (or blame), with the other four members of the band acting as mere foils for his psychodrama. There was no lowering of the bar. He took one step off the ledge.

Anderson's 2015 "Letter of Recommendation" confirms that the album (remastered and marketed in deluxe editions with outtakes and alternates) is still being evaluated. At the time of its release, Stephen Holden of Rolling Stone criticised Tusk in semi-inspired prose: "If the band has an image, it's one of wealthy, talented, bohemian cosmopolites futilely toying with shopworn romantic notions in the face of the void." He said of Nicks, "There's a fine line between exotic and bizarre." She was neither, and there is no fine line, but the absence he mentions is a remnant of the album. Looking back three and a half decades, Amanda Petrusich makes us wonder if all that upbeat studio footage and cheerful twirling in the sun at Dodger Stadium was a ruse.

By the time Tusk was released, the band's two primary relationships (Christine and John's marriage and Lindsey and Stevie's long-standing romance) had completely disintegrated, proving Fleetwood Mac to be one of our best and brave chroniclers of love's horrifying tumult. Being asked to perform background vocals for a song written about you by your ex-lover months (and eventually years) after the relationship has ended? Keep in mind how painful that must have been.

Despite the pain, the five musicians stayed together for a long time, with their label, promoters and producers, hundreds of employees in their entourage, shareholders and boards of trustees—an entire sector of commercial entertainment—reminding them, along with lawyers and dealers, that hundreds of millions of dollars were at stake. We should also consider how much pressure there must have been before, during, and after Tusk's avant-garde crackdown, and how private, intimate, and discreet topics are still shamefully publicised for profit.

Hernan Rojas, producer and engineer Ken Caillat's assistant, exacerbated the agony by falling in love with Nicks (as detailed in their record book), while Christine McVie had an affair with Beach Boys member Dennis Wilson. (As a side note, while Brian Wilson had a much greater creative influence on Fleetwood Mac than his brother Dennis, the band did record a cover of Dennis's "Farmer's Daughter" in 1963. Despite being recorded in the studio, it ended up on the Fleetwood Mac Live album in 1980, not Tusk.) Both Fleetwood and Buckingham had lost their fathers while working on Tusk, and they both had serious health issues. Fleetwood checked out, but Buckingham was constantly checking in. He recorded several versions of "I Know I'm Not Wrong" at home, each no worse or better than the previous one. He captured the text's inconsistencies in music by coarsening the sound after smoothing it, alternately growling and cooing into the microphone, and unplugging and returning the instruments: "The dreams of a lifetime / A year gone bad." Nicks was ready to work, but her ex-partner took complete control of the project, resulting in a purposefully uneven record that begins with "Over & Over" and ends with "Never Forget." Christine McVie's bookends are respectful. The remainder isn't.

Tusk's excesses have been widely publicised, but its treatment of popular music history has received less attention. It pays homage to the Beatles' White Album's bric-a-brac and longueurs, the Beach Boys', Talking Heads', and everything Buckingham liked about punk, as well as Cowell- and Cage-style ultramodernism. It's an antidote to the anaemic musical culture of Los Angeles' Laurel Canyon, which, with fewer people than eucalyptus trees in its prime, served as a haven for folk and rock performers, their hangers-on, and their pothead pop offspring. The area lacked the coherence of a "scene," but it produced (or was credited with producing) a floating, mushy sound and a hazy mood that critics dislike.

Nicks wrote five of the songs on Tusk, and their sophistication adds depth to the story of dissolute, out-of-it self-destruction. She contributed "Angel," a reimagining of a "old-time dance hall girl" song; the luxurious, immersive "Sara"; the devastating ballad "Storms"; the astral anthem "Sisters of the Moon," whose lyrics perplex even the author; and "Beautiful Child," which demonstrates Nicks' voice deepening and enriching. None of the songs mentioned Buckingham, either as a person or as an artist. She went her way, and he followed the frame tracks.

The recorded version of "Angel" is slower than how the band performed it on tour in 1979, when it exploded with Nicks' clever footwork and vamping outro. Buckingham laid down the rhythm with overdrive on a custom-made Turner guitar, which he used on tour rather than in the studio for Tusk. He used custom-built Les Paul and Stratocaster guitars there. The song has a bouncy boogie woogie foundation (root and sixth notes alternate with an eighth-note baseline). Buckingham's fills glide over that beat, following the lyrics in a distinct manner. A guitarist who is less creative and sensitive is more likely to strut and rely on blues clichés. Buckingham avoids showiness throughout Tusk, instead opting for a filigreed fingerpicking style that is pianistic in the sense that the right hand thumb plays bass parts (similar to the left hand of a piano) while the fingers play chordal arpeggiations, melodies, and fills.

According to footage from one of the recording sessions, Buckingham and Nicks struggled in the studio to achieve the two-part harmony of the song's chorus. Nicks makes a genuine attempt to compare the harmonies to those of the Mills Brothers, an African American jazz quartet who rose to prominence during the Great Depression and remained popular into the 1950s. Nobody pays attention. Nicky finally raises her hands. "Nobody understands what I'm even saying," she complains, shaking her head as the men continue to chat. Buckingham remains at the piano when they resume, trailing Nicks in thirds beneath her line until he shifts obliquely with a passing fourth and a couple of sixths. In some ways, the entire song is a continuation of the free shift. The chorus is removed less than halfway through, creating an unusual structure: v1 chorus, v2 chorus, v3 v2 v4, and outro. Perhaps stanza 2 is the true chorus, or perhaps the song is intended to be performed improvised in a Badlands saloon. The interaction and synthesis of rhythm and rhyme, set against the steady beat and bustling bass, is fascinating. The lyrics, like the harmonic underpinning—three block chords, the dominant, subdominant, and tonic of G major—are snappy, and the vocabulary is incomprehensibly concise. The upbeat tune complements a text about deep love that has turned cold between newfound strangers. Each speaks or appears to speak: You are in a good mood. I found it amusing that you received it because I knew you would. You were exceptional when you were at your best.

In verse two, the chorus lines are followed by a mystical reference to Rhiannon's story and the figure of Arawn, "the great lord of darkness," whose touch induces endless sleep: "So I close my eyes softly / Till I become that part of the wind." According to Nicks, the wind represents breath, mentality, and inspiration, while the song is about the bliss of painless slumber and the gift of death. "And in that nonexistence of pain, there will be happiness." Because it was presented with great affection. And this was in a ghostly song, at a magical hour, and this was the angel... of my dreams." The music corresponds to the lyrics about shape shifting.

CHAPTER 4
FLEETWOOD MAC

In his book Get Tusked, producer and engineer Ken Caillat describes the band's jumbled conversations from four decades ago with astonishing precision and clarity. Perhaps Caillat and his collaborator, Hernan Rojas, took detailed notes or secretly recorded the studio banter while working with Fleetwood Mac. Caillat describes the atmosphere in Studio D as stressful at the beginning of the book; the band, or what remains of it after the Rumours tour, is unable to get its act together or even show up on time, but Caillat's concerns are short-lived. From Santa Monica to Malibu, he drives his Ferrari along the Pacific Coast Highway. Aeroplanes land at LAX.

In his rented fantasy house on Big Rock Mesa, he will discover chilled champagne and a discarded leotard. He's in his thirties, and Cheryl, his 21-year-old lover, is waiting for him in the pool. A soft-porn scene ensues. Caillat also talks about microphones, amplifiers, and the specifics of songs like "Sara," Tusk's second single. Nicks worked with musician and producer Tom "Tommy Rude" Moncrieff to record a first draft on a cassette player, then added a second layer of singing to the playback. Bob Aguirre, a founding member of Fritz, recorded the demo at his home studio in Bel Air. She brought the song into Studio D on December 9, 1978, six months into the fifteen-month process of recording and mastering the album (June 21, 1978–September 30, 1979). Rojas used a Roland TR-77 drum machine to create a minimalist arrangement of the original piano-vocal. Moncrieff played bass (on a Fender Precision bass in the style of John McVie), while Annie McLoone provided backing vocals. (McLoone sang with Nicks and Buckingham on Walter Egan's "Magnet and Steel.") Acoustic guitar and richer vocal harmonies followed. Fleetwood replaced the beatbox line with his own, which inspired McVie's bass line. The bass drum and floor tom thuds were amplified as the kit was adjusted down. The traditional process of shortening and tightening the structure began, but Nicks objected to the production team's changes, lamenting the loss of verse after verse: "I was to the point where I went, 'Is the word Sara even going to be left in the song?'" Caillat confirms that "the buck stopped with me" regarding the budget cuts.Initially, Lindsey would help me with the cuts, but later on, I would work with Stevie to reduce the lyrics and trim the fat, often while she cried. Of course, Hernan's affair with her exacerbated the situation!"

"Sara" was originally sixteen minutes long, but Rojas cut it to thirteen and then eleven minutes. Later, at Caillat's request, the song was edited to 8:49 (beginning with Nicks saying, "I wanna be a star / I don't want to be a cleaning lady"), before being cut to 6:22 for release. (The single is much shorter, coming in at 4:41.) Rojas was correct to be concerned about destroying the master by cutting it before rather than after a downbeat. Manual edits were used, with the tape marked with a white pencil and "rocked" to the appropriate location between the tape reels for the excision. Once the operation was completed successfully, Rojas pitched the song to Caillat and Dashut, the album's second producer, before presenting it to Buckingham, who saw its potential and began working on it. Caillat recorded his guitar performance, which added the final layer of polish to the song, with three microphones. One routed the music through a "fat box" into the console, while the other used a Mesa/Boogie California Tweed amplifier, which has become synonymous with iconic overdriven sounds. The third microphone, a Sony EMC50 lavalier, was "taped under the strings between the pickups to capture the subtle string work," which is an extremely unusual method for finding a new tone. (Caillat first used the lavalier in this way on Joni Mitchell's Miles of Aisles live album in 1974.) Buckingham intended to create a delicate and fragile latticework of strumming, jangling, and off-kilter, slightly out-of-tune rhythmic plinking hidden deep in the mix. With the piano lines, the guitar section absorbed five or six stereo recordings. Buckingham's sounds are interlaced or braided over McVie's circular bass pattern and Fleetwood's brushstrokes, as the title implies.

Fleetwood as the "great dark wing"; Don Henley or another partner, John David Souther, "undoing the laces" of a chemise; and Sara as the singer's alter ego or a child Nicks never had do not completely persuade. Such interpretations resemble the blurbs on the cover of a bodice ripper: "forbidden passion," "a darker intrigue," and "fortunes change and reputations—even lives—are jeopardised." Either Nicks saw herself as a character in such a novel, or something more sinister is at work. She has downplayed rumours about the personal parts on occasion, telling Entertainment Weekly in 2009 that the song was not about model and singer Sara Recor, "who was one of my best friends—even though everybody thinks it is." Recor, for her part, recalls sitting with Nicks while working on the song and believes it refers to events in both her and Nicks' lives, particularly their practically inextricably linked sexual experiences with Fleetwood. According to Record, Nicks "changes her thoughts" about its contents and meaning "depending on how she feels about me, and the others involved." In 2009, Nicks' feelings about Record were conflicted because so much had happened in their lives.

I used her name because I adore it, but the story was about what was going on in our lives at the time. It was about Mick and my relationship, as well as the one I started after Mick. Some songs are about a lot of things, while others only have one or two lines that are the main idea, and the rest is just like making a movie, writing a plot around that one paragraph, that little kernel of life. "When you build your house" means that when you get your act together, please let me know, because I truly cannot be around you until you do.

The ambiguity could explain the tense variations in the lyrics. In verses 1 and 2, the narrator addresses her lover in the first person, and Sara becomes an addressee in chorus 2. Then there are the oscillations: the lover has left but the love stays, or the lover has left but the love remains; the song confirms closure, then denies it; "call me home" identifies a gap in the form as a double entendre. Is "drowning in the sea of love" the best description of Nicks' haphazard partner swapping if the lyrics had any real meaning in Nicks' life? Except for the 1979 St. Louis performance, in which she emphasises the emotional significance of the outro lyric "There's a heartbeat that never really dies" by repeating it, the demos and archived performed versions provide little clarity. Her movement between microphones and instruments stands out as a visual acknowledgement of the song's discursive nature, even in its most stripped-down form.

Tack piano, also known as jangle piano, is a standard piano modified with tacks or nails to produce the old-time, out-of-tune sound of a saloon upright. It's a marvellously refined stylization of the piano playing on the rough draft, which Nicks replicated on an unpublished

VH1 Storytellers show. She reclaims authorship from Buckingham and the producers midway through a minute of mediocre honky-tonk: "I did write it." Two tack-piano tracks are panned on opposite sides, resulting in arpeggios similar to guitar or dulcimer, but with a greater percussive impact. McVie and Fleetwood's groove begins. Even as they advance a melodic hook, the words remain misty. Much of the beauty comes from the silky, breathy production and the wonderful textural response to the strain of the lyrics, which begin with the half-minute protraction of "And undoing / and undoing... the laces." Sensuality is sacrificed in favour of lost innocence and emotional betrayal. The three background vocal lines, which swirl around each other before drifting down and apart, represent both the lacework and its destruction. The lines end with exhaled repeats of the title word, "Sa-ra." Throughout, there are anticlimaxes, such as Nick singing "home" far back in the mix after the line "But when you build your house / Then call me."

"Sisters of the Moon" is darker, harsher, and frantic. The title could refer to nighttime deities in pagan rituals, but no one (including Nicks) knows if that was her intention. Nicks' stylist, Margi Kent, made her a necklace with a triangular pendant representing "sisterhood & continuity," or the unbroken existence of goddesses, which I assumed was the song's meaning. I sought confirmation from a practising witch, Kristen Sollée, who said, "The title is certainly evocative of the mythological connections between the moon and the witch, the divine feminine." Ancient Greek and Roman lunar goddesses such as Hecate and Diana were incorporated into late mediaeval and early modern witchcraft lore, which was revived and reframed by occultists and feminists in the nineteenth and twentieth centuries for their own political and spiritual purposes, so when I listen to that song, I am reminded of the serpentine path of witch history."

The lyrics include numerous spiritual references. When she sings "Sisters," Nicks is a whirling, serenading person of higher calling who embodies the "spirit of sexual espièglerie" (to quote cultural historian Perry Anderson).The tune is similar to "Rhiannon," but the texture at the beginning is similar to "Gold Dust Woman," implying that the psychoactive is working alongside the paranormal. "Sisters" makes reference to thresholds, doppelgangers, metamorphosis, and the "dark at the top of the stairs," implying a journey into and out of the realm of the dead. Fleetwood Mac wrote "Sisters," like "Tusk," while on tour, and the second lyric may refer to fan demands: "The people, they love her / And still they are the cruellest."

The title appears on the fourth line, rather than gradually building up over the verses and satisfying the listener when it arrives. Fleetwood's kick drum and clamping hi-hat create a mesmerising pulse, while Nicks adds intriguing "oohs" in the background. The layered background vocals and Nicks' line "and she called to me" are out of sync. This song and "Sara," according to Rolling Stone's Stephen Holden, "weave personal symbolism and offbeat mythology into a near impenetrable murk." This remark perplexed Stephen Davis, who described Nicks's song "Sisters" in his book as "more of a mood than an actual song." Davis likens it to "a famous series of watercolours from the 1930s" by the English-born Mexican artist Leonora Carrington, which featured "idealised magical heroines and spiritual intermediaries such as Diana the Huntress, Fantasia, Iris, the goddess Rumour," and, derogatorily and redundantly, "the Gypsy queen Indovina Zingara."

During their Tusk tour in 1979-80, Fleetwood Mac performed the song in supernatural mode. The "Sisters" footage begins with backstage shots of each member preparing for the show. Buckingham is in the mirror fixing his hair, Christine McVie is sitting cross-legged smoking a cigarette, Nicks is also touching up her hair, and Fleetwood gasps for air and even puts on an oxygen mask. Nicks, dressed in a black stole, kicks off the song by hitting a cowbell with a drumstick. After the verses and choruses, Nicks yells the lyric "Know my name, yeah!" as Buckingham begins the violent parts of his solo. The lights go out, followed by a burst of bright whites and yellow. As the audience grows louder, Nicks sings with her hand raised. She grabs the microphone stand, reaches out to the audience, and mouths something inaudible before bending down as the lights go out. Buckingham's guitar enhances her vocal power on this occasion.

The verses of "Sisters" are in A minor, F major 7, G major, and A minor, with the power chord riff in A minor, G major, E minor, F major, G major, and A minor. This pattern may have been put to rest by Led Zeppelin's "Stairway to Heaven" (1971), but it reappeared during rock music's Season of the Witch. The song is structured as follows: a meandering intro, two verses punctuated by the riff, a bridge, and a blazing guitar solo as an outro. The solo fades out on the album but ends abruptly and raggedly on the 2002 remaster.

Caillat claims that the band worked on the song for 36 takes in a friendly environment, but he overlooks the rather inconvenient fact that Walter Egan had been playing a different harmonised version of the song on the road under the name "Sister," with Nicks' permission, and had planned to record it on his second album. Buckingham stopped him "out of disdain" because Egan was "connecting with his former partner."

Hearing it now, it's difficult to imagine it as a song written specifically for Egan: the sound is so Fleetwood Mac, with multiple guitars melting into a whole greater than the sum of its parts. In comparison, Egan's music is riff-driven, whereas Fleetwood Mac's is not, with Caillat focusing on filigreed textures. He transformed "Sisters" into an excellent example of stereo envisioning, which compensates for the syntax's brevity. One guitar starts on the right, playing light fills; another strums in the middle; and another joins on the right, with more processing and a hint of chorus. Finally, the most assertive guitar appears on the left, but it is set to become the overdriven solo line. Various levels of reverb add depth to the stereo field. The solo on the left is repeated and panned to the right, resulting in a hazy effect. The song starts desolate and ends with a primal scream.

"Beautiful Child" is also from an "astral plane," but it is stripped down rather than built up, and the proportions are appropriate for the subject. Like "Sara," it may allude to the mother Nicks never was, reflecting not so much (or solely) on her reproductive choices as on her creative energies—her ability to birth and nurture her own inspiration to maturity. Nicks has stated that her affair with Beatles publicity officer Derek Taylor inspired "Beautiful Child". (Add that to the long list of Fleetwood Mac love affairs, this time revealed long after the fact and detachedly, as if the affair and the song were about someone else—the artist from four decades ago.) Taylor was sixteen years her senior and married, so their liaisons at the Beverly Hills Hotel had to be kept secret and ended in a stalemate.

The lyrics also discuss dealing with life-or-death issues, father-daughter issues, being treated as a child in emotionally and psychologically harmful situations, and growing up and maturing as a natural process rather than an option. "Are you too trusting?" The key connection is "Yes / But then women usually are." The song begins as a barbeque, rocking on the piano between two pitches in the right hand and three in the left, twinkling like the stars. The structure is hazy, but it boils down to three interconnected chords—F major 7, G major 6, and A minor—that drift apart throughout the arrangement, resulting in a larger void. As the performance demonstrates, the astral element depicts Tusk as a labour of love with a hole in its heart. The snare drum sound is reversed so that the assault's resonance appears before the attack itself on its first entry; the bass guitar section is synthesised an octave lower. As the texture becomes hollowed out, it expands. Nicks, Buckingham, and Christine McVie sing in the background, and their tracks were recorded separately in a reverb-heavy live environment. The song's ending brings them together in a subtle, cloaked eeriness.

Some hear Brian Wilson's unreleased album Smile, but it's actually less noticeable here than on Buckingham's ballads "That's All for Everyone" and "Walk a Thin Line." Both are masterpieces of dovetailed, overlapping vocal harmony, capping a legacy that includes the Beach Boys, Beatles, Four Freshmen, jazz, and blues. The surround-sound experience of "Beautiful Child" highlights minor differences in the voices' apparent absorption. It's a Derridean trick: the unspoken and unheard cannot be reduced to the same concept. Indeed, when Nicks sings "Your hands, held mine for so few hours," McVie adds an unconnected sentence over a cadence: "I fell into love." Following that, starting at 3:33 in the original version, the backing vocalists sing Nicks' previous lyrics. She swears she "will do as I'm told," but voices in the distance and in her head tell her otherwise. She isn't a child anymore. The album's closing track, Christine McVie's "Never Forget," depicts a Malibu sunrise following the last pool party of the era. The tone she was attempting to establish is undone by "ennui." Caillat's expanded version includes electronic treatments that are abruptly terminated. The needle drops on a seductive double record made by an alcoholic, dissolute, and checked-out band. The end result is hilarious, tragic, profound, bizarre, ground-down, built-up, perforated, and lavishly padded. In contrast, the marching band marches in a specific position to accommodate the microphones. Nicks was offended enough by the moniker Tusk to threaten to leave the band. She had previously threatened to do so with regard to "Silver Springs." She would soon. Outside of Fleetwood Mac, Nicks and Buckingham were in high demand, the former for her singing and the latter for his production abilities. Consider their collaboration with John Stewart on "Gold," Stewart's biggest hit that was unmistakable on the radio in 1979. Stewart, who was largely unknown outside of the US folk circuit, released ten albums with the Kingston Trio's second lineup. The House Un-American Activities Committee (HUAC) did not investigate the Kingston Trio, despite previously investigating the Weavers and Pete Seeger for communist sympathies. The Weavers were a group of idealistic leftists who believed their music could expose white American middle-class audiences to "other" cultures. McCarthyites deemed the attempt dangerous and seditious, prompting Seeger's appearance before HUAC in August 1955 and his First Amendment defence. Two complex portrayals of the "roots" of American folk festivals and their politics, Robert Cantwell's When We Were Good and Benjamin Filene's Romancing the Folk, demonstrate that their use of suppressed communities' music constituted an unashamed cultural appropriation. The Kingston Trio was perfectly groomed, blond, blue-eyed, WASP, and all-American. The trio popularised folk music, particularly the classic bluegrass gambling song "Little Maggie," for a larger audience. Stewart toured incessantly and lived respectably, if not extravagantly, after contributing to the Monkees' massive hit "Daydream Believer" in 1967. He was a San Diego native, the son of a horse trainer (he credits his rhythms to hoofbeats), and had been playing guitar and banjo since he was a toddler. Johnny Cash held a special place in his record collection. He sang rock 'n' roll in the shower but ballads about the elements (especially wind and fire) on tour. After the Kingston Trio broke up in 1967, he and vocalist Buffy Ford toured the country in support of Robert F. Kennedy's presidential campaign, playing in school gymnasiums, train cars, and truck beds. John F. Kennedy was assassinated on June 5, 1968, at the Ambassador Hotel in Los Angeles; Stewart responded with the cult album California Bloodlines, a collection of autobiographical observations and past compositions influenced by John Steinbeck and Jack Kerouac. The Kingston Trio provided the musical backdrop for Nicks and Buckingham's early years together. When they first met, Nicks screamed at Stewart, "If you knew how many hundreds of hours Lindsey made me sit and listen to your albums!," referring to Buckingham's guitar-playing style, which was influenced by the Kingston Trio. In 1979, the musical recipient was given the opportunity to repay the donor. Stewart had signed with RSO and was hoping for gold. Maybe he'll find a hit. He attended the Tusk recording sessions and noticed a distant Kingston Trio influence in the banjo-style guitar playing on the toe tapper "That's Enough for Me." RSO was sceptical of Stewart's ability to produce a hit record on his own and rejected numerous song revisions; "no hits here," RSO president Al Coury declared. Buckingham took over, but the $100,000 production budget had already been spent. Buckingham answered Stewart's request by donating both his time and money to the initiative. He was listed as a co-producer on the album "Bombs Away Dream Babies," which included "Gold," a song about attempting to compose a popular song that became a hit, as well as two other singles: "Midnight Wind" and "Lost Her in the Sun." "Gold" is almost identical to one of Walter Egan's best compositions, "Hot Summer Nights," which he wrote to replace "Sisters of the Moon" after Buckingham confiscated it for Tusk (clearly with Nicks' sayo). Stewart and Egan were acquaintances, and Stewart had told Egan at the Local 47 musicians' union in Los Angeles that he planned to write a song similar to "Hot Summer Nights." He certainly did. Egan may have had a case of copyright infringement, but he did not pursue it, and "Gold" peaked at number five on the Billboard charts.

It was Stewart's second number-one single. The first, he told a London interviewer in 1979, was "Midnight Wind." Buckingham "and [keyboardist] Joey Carbone and [drummer] Russ Kunkel came down and played on 'Midnight Wind.'... Yeah, it was the best birthday I'd ever had.""We got drunk out of our heads." It was not a hit, and Nicks advised him to improve his performance for "Gold." Stewart remembers their conversation in a different light, reducing her musical ability to serving his desires. "John," she allegedly said, "make it so it turns you on." Because it will not turn them on unless it first turns you on. Because they aren't any different than you. The gold in "Gold" is a shuffle Stewart created backstage between shows, combined with the internal rhymes of a children's song: down/town, car/guitar. The appeal is threefold: "California girls," "each one a song in the making"; the sensation of driving along the Pacific Coast Highway just before dawn, well over the alcohol limit, everything blurred; and the pursuit of fame. Stewart grew up in Malibu and refers to the "California town" of Agoura Hills, as well as Kanan Road, which connects Thousand Oaks and Malibu via the Ventura Freeway. Stewart had hired Nicks as a backup singer for "Midnight Wind," but he did not have the funds to bring her on board for "Gold." Fortunately, Nicks had brought her girlfriend Mary Torrey into the studio:

So when [Nicks] came down that night to perform "Midnight Wind," I pulled out "Gold" and pretended I was mixing it or something. The expression on her face as she walked in told me she was not going to sing that night. She just had that "I ain't singing" look on her face. That's the reason why I said, "Stevie, I'm gonna do the tag on this song—let's you and Mary and I go out [to the live room] and sing the end." So Mary began crying, and I thought, "Oh, my God, what did I say?" "John," Stevie explained, "this is Mary's dream to sing on a record." I said, "We've got to go out and do it." So we went outside to play tag while Mary sang and cried. Stevie can't see very well, so I had the lyrics to "Gold" typed out on large cue cards. "Stevie, come on, let's just do the verses of this song," I suggested as Mary returned to the booth. "It should not take long." "Turn the tape on," I yelled, and they did. I put my hand over Stevie's mouth when she wasn't supposed to sing and hit her in the back when she was, and she did it in one take, and I got her on the song. Stewart takes pleasure in his abuse because he believes Nicks tolerated it. She may not have had the authority or desire to ruin his career at the time, but she could have walked out of the studio. Instead, she sings without conviction and gradually falls behind the beat, making her voice audible to all. After leaving folk music's Eden for rock's badlands, the prodigal son composed his prodigal song. Stewart achieved his peak by lip-syncing it on the music show Solid Gold, just before Blondie and

Supertramp performed. RSO hired him for another album, Dream Babies Go Hollywood, which was a disaster. The more upscale venues stopped inviting him to perform. He had never seen anything like Nicks' vast swaths of upturned, adoring faces. Stewart rejected "Gold" and returned to recording folk records under his own label, Homecoming, and performing in small venues in front of his devoted fans. He and Buffy Ford married, with each serving as the other's muse while writing songs. Stewart died from Alzheimer's disease in 2008, but not before making another disparaging remark about Nicks: "A lot of people think Stevie Nicks is really nuts." She isn't; she has simply discovered or created a way for herself to function in the appropriate lobe. Then, too late, he admits something true, borne of resentment rather than admiration: "She's one of the most underrated songwriters in America."

"the goldfish and the ladybug"

Fleetwood Mac disbanded after the Tusk tour, dissatisfied with having performed almost everywhere except the Soviet Union. Politics student John McVie expressed an interest in visiting the Soviet Union, and Mick Fleetwood and the others were intrigued. The Soviets would have had a difficult time satisfying the contract rider for the high-maintenance band, but the idea of a show in Moscow had been discussed since 1977, with backing from the White House, the US State Department, and the Russian Embassy in Washington, DC. Embassy employees received complimentary tickets to see the band perform in Landover, Maryland, as well as an invitation to an after-party hosted by the United Nations and Warner Brothers. "Anyone who saw those Russians clutching their Fleetwood Mac albums to be autographed, clustered around sexy lead singer Stevie Nicks like bees to honeysuckle, could sense there was hope for the future of détente," according to an Associated Press report on July 15, 1977. According to lawyer Mickey Shapiro, the Soviets admired the band's "cleanliness," and the embassy's outspoken press counsellor, Valentin Kamenev, backed the idea of a television broadcast of Fleetwood Mac performing in Red Square, with proceeds going to UNESCO. Kamenev asked for a crate of Rumours copies as a gift for the bureaucrats back home. Shapiro recalls travelling to Moscow in the dead of winter for three days of meetings with chain-smoking, tea-drinking officials, following which he inspected television facilities and received a letter of intent for a performance in the vast Rossiya Hotel's music hall near Red Square. However, the matter has been postponed. Both geopolitical tensions and the band's volume needed to be reduced at first. The Soviet invasion of Afghanistan, combined with the United States' withdrawal from the 1980 Moscow Olympics, effectively ended the project. Nicks' post-Tusk ambitions included a musical, ballet, film, and a collection of stories, including her fairytale "The Golden Fox of the Last Fox Hunt." Don Henley, the Eagles' drummer, introduced her to manager, producer, and entertainment expert Irving Azoff, a brilliant but often erratic businessman. "To get top dollar for his clients, he'll rip up contracts, yell, scream, terrorise, stomp, pound, and destroy inanimate objects... gleefully." "He is the American Dream taken by the balls," Cameron Crowe fumed about him in 1978, recounting an incident in which Azoff unleashed his rage on the walls of a hotel room using a chainsaw. Azoff agreed to be Nicks' manager after she enlisted the help of Paul Fishkin and Danny Goldberg to form an independent label for her solo work, which would be distributed by Atlantic rather than Warner Brothers. Fishkin had previously collaborated with Todd Rundgren and Warner's Bearsville Records label, while Goldberg had worked with Led Zeppelin and Atlantic's Swan Song. Both were in Nicks' circle of friends and confidants; she and Fishkin started dating after meeting at a record business convention; they agreed that Fleetwood Mac had not properly acknowledged her. Mick's pushy attitude toward Nicks in business irritated her. She sought advice from Margi Kent, Robin Snyder, and Herbert Worthington, the photographer who designed the "white album" and Rumours covers. It was a watershed moment in her career, personally, creatively, and financially, as she was caught in the middle of discussions between Fleetwood Mac, Mick's desire to negotiate a solo agreement for her that he could control, and her own team.

Goldberg met Nicks "in '77 or '78," and the two became friends and remained in touch "even after she and Fishkin split up."He recalls "running a public relations firm, and Bearsville, which Fishkin was president of, was a client." Goldberg, on the opposite end of the spectrum, had "aspirations to do other things in the business," while Nicks, on the opposite end of the spectrum, "initially asked me for some PR advice about how to get Margi Kent, who designed her clothes, into Vogue (I was unable to deliver); then I worked with her to try to get a movie made based on Rhiannon—a film that was never made but on the development of which we worked for more than a year." Goldberg recalls eating tacos in Nicks' kitchen while listening to her work on potential film music on her Bösendorfer piano. "Her intuitive writing style captivated him.She'd sit at the piano for hours, zone out, and then write a song. Stevie's mysticism stemmed solely from within. Rimbaud, Blake, and Ginsberg studies, as well as the Bible, did not appeal to her. She was a self-taught mystic who saw the world from the perspective of a middle-class American. Later, he went with her to Tucson to see Evangeline Walton. Goldberg proposed Rhiannon to several studios. Unfortunately, it did not make any progress. "There was a deal with United Artists films—I was a 'producer' and then 'co producer' with someone who had actually produced movies, named Rob Cohen," he went on to explain. "A screenwriter named Paul Mayersberg (known for The Man Who Fell to Earth) was hired to write a draft, which did not impress the studio, and that was that."Another concept, "an animated TV special based on an unreleased song Stevie had written called 'The Goldfish and the Ladybug,'" was floated, but it did not make it beyond a "development deal at ABC TV." The conversation turned back to her desire for a creative break from Fleetwood Mac, as well as an independent recording, production, and distribution agreement. Goldberg founded Modern Records specifically for her. Nicks dreaded telling Mick Fleetwood the news, but learning about his romance with her friend Sara Recor made it a lot easier.

CHAPTER 5
BELLA DONNA

Irving Azoff's successful segment of the market included the Eagles, Steely Dan, and other chart-topping artists. He had a star for the 1980s in Stevie Nicks on Modern Records, but bringing her into the new decade would require changing her sound and image, as well as musically moving out of California and into the white working-class heartland. Experimentation, suaveness, and a style "speaks not of roots but of a lack of them" had to go. Her debut solo album effectively asks Fleetwood Mac fans to reconsider their listening habits. Fewer dreams, increased awareness of life's deceptions.

She originally named it Belladonna, after the poisonous nightshade plant that has long been associated with magic and spiritual rituals, but later changed it to Bella Donna. He reminds her that he had warned her about the "possible backlash about naming her album after a [highly toxic] psychedelic, and she changed it to Bella Donna, which she said was what she always had in mind because it meant 'beautiful dancer.'" The cover is a tribute to the past while also representing a fresh start. In a white gown and extremely high heels, she looks into the camera, her gold bracelet glinting in the bulb's flash. Maxwellington, her brother's cockatoo, sits on her uplifted, oddly folded right hand. A shrine of white roses, a translucent tambourine, and a crystal ball are at her feet. Nicks collaborated with Jimmy Iovine, a sound engineer and producer before becoming an all-powerful record executive, to record it. Iovine collaborated with John Lennon on three albums before moving on to work with Bruce Springsteen, Patti Smith (on the epic song "Because the Night"), U2, Eminem, and, most importantly for Nicks, Tom Petty, who would join the ranks of the extras in her career, an occasional influencer whose hustle, prematurely grizzled voice, and torn-up sound she dug. On December 8, 1980, John Lennon was assassinated, which stunned and appalled both Iovine and Nicks. When interviewed for stories about corporate movers and shakers, Iovine taught humility—not believing one's own BS—but he has led an alpha-male existence, capitalising on great ideas, overcoming obstacles, and stepping on others. He was introduced to Nicks by Paul Fishkin and Goldberg, and he hardened Nicks' voice, facilitating her long-awaited departure from Fleetwood Mac. Her manager, Azoff, and his partner, Howard Kaufman, accepted the transfer. Annie Zaleski's outstanding account of the making of Bella Donna and its 2016 deluxe re-release includes sessions with Nicks and two Fleetwood Mac backup vocalists. The two of them began to meet "in the living room of a rented oceanside home, working out harmonies and singing together while the album's musical director, Benmont Tench (keyboardist with Tom Petty and the Heartbreakers), added accompaniment." Iovine then started his task. For the studio sessions, he enlisted "a slew of hotshot male musicians, including members of the Heartbreakers, the E Street Band, and the Eagles." Waddy Wachtel (and, on occasion, Mike Campbell) delivered scorching guitar licks, while Russ Kunkel's soothing percussion, Tench's lush organ, and Roy Bittan's pensive piano provided depth."

Nicks' songs lament a lack of resolve and weigh the consequences of unrestrained desire. The method is intended to be imperceptible; the fragility of shape and line becomes an expressive power. Some lines appear to be autobiographical, but only in vague terms; memory plays tricks. Petty sings more genetically about broken promises, luck running out, and pride giving way to grief. The comments won him over to Johnny Cash, who wrote him a letter describing him as "a good man to ride the river with." His music is efficient and concentrated, full of sequences, brighter than Nicks' (though he was a melancholy, truculent sort in person), and populated by southerners and feisty gals. Guitar playing varies from rough to crisp. When MTV came along, his videos became more rebellious and unusual. Nicks took a little longer to adjust to the medium.

"She came into my life like a rocket, just refusing to go away," Petty said of Nicks, conveniently ignoring the fact that when she expressed interest in leaving Fleetwood Mac for his band in the late 1970s, Doug Morris, the head of Atlantic Records, informed her that Petty did not allow women in the Heartbreakers. Their first meeting was a flop because Petty was uncomfortable with Nicks' "sisterhood" of "hangers-on." "We never had guests in the studio," he said. "It seemed strange to me." Nonetheless, he admired her voice because it complemented his fragile-forceful country-rock sound. Iovine was his producer, and he became hers as well, which irritated Petty after Iovine and Nicks briefly became romantically involved. Petty was concerned that Iovine would prefer Nicks' music over his own. After staying with Iovine, Nicks moved into her home for a while, staying out of sight when Petty came over to record material for his album Hard Promises (1981). Petty was in great shape at the time, and the album came together quickly. Songs that were partially or entirely composed by other musicians did not make the final cut.

Wachtel's guitar riff on "Edge of Seventeen" tests a musician's stamina: two measures of palm-muted, quickly played sixteenths on the root of E minor, followed by measures on C and D, repeated. "Bring on the Night," a Police song, served as inspiration. Wachtel added a dotted eighth note delay and a slow-moving modulation effect with chorus. (Here, police guitarist Andy Summers prefers phasers.) The four-measure ostinato plays throughout the 5:28 song, starting with a firmly closed hi-hat and moving back for the vocal, drum, and piano entrances. Iovine reintroduces the ostinato at the 3:11 break before the final chorus, revealing or exposing the song's primordial core. In the bridge, the piano mimics the guitar by dribbling on E and C and cycling through the same trio of chords in various inversions. Nicks begins the first stanza by attacking the range from i to V of E minor. The subsequent "ooh ooh ooh" relieves the pressure by floating down from G via F# to the tonic. The rhythm is repeated, the drums enter, and the pressure rises once more. It's a furiously captivating song, with tremendous unison backup singing (a far cry from Fleetwood Mac), offbeat Stewart Copeland-inspired "bombs" in the bass drum and cymbal, fluttering piano flourishes, and the powerful vocal interjection "everything sucks" behind Nicks's "nothing else matters."

The outcome was significant for Petty, who referred to her as "one of the premiere songwriters of our time" due to her authenticity. In his account, Danny Goldberg backs up Petty's claim. "Edge of Seventeen," on the other hand, brings back painful memories for him. Despite his lack of filmmaking experience, he suggested filming the video himself, claiming that "Stevie's own environment, filled with cosmic drawings and knickknacks, and her own private flamboyance would be a great visual accompaniment to the song." The result was "unflattering" and needed to be "scrapped" in favour of footage from her HBO performance of the song. Goldberg felt humbled; Nicks forgave him, and the song went viral.

Nicks named Bella Donna after her grandfather, A.J. "I can't believe that the next life couldn't be better than this," she wrote in Rolling Stone a month after the album came out. "If it isn't, I don't want to know." If you're reincarnated, I believe you'll be reincarnated as many times as you want—once you've cleared your karma and office. I believe my grandfather is very close right now; otherwise, I would not have included country music on my record. I try not to overthink things, but I believe it will be easier in the next life.

The album's country music is an imagined memory of A.J.'s gin-mill appearances. Michael Little mocked it so tenderly that Nicks couldn't be offended, even if he misses the point about the specific female audience she's addressing in her words, among the odes to imposter syndrome and, for A.J., the feeling that you'll never make it. "After the Glitter Fades" has such a "Rhinestone Cowboy" vibe to it that Glen Campbell felt compelled to cover it, and for good reason; it's genuine El Lay Country Glam right down to Nicks' "Well, I never thought I'd make it here in Hollywood." And Nicks transforms country lament "The Highwayman" into witchy "Haute Couture and Western" lyrics like "Her horse is like a dragonfly / She is just a fool." I can hear Hank Williams Jr. singing the song, but not the lyrics, if that makes sense.

True, Campbell recorded "After the Glitter Fades," but Nicks imagined Dolly Parton performing the song in the 1970s. "It was sent to her, but I don't think Dolly ever received it." "I believe she would have wanted to perform the song if she had received it." Parton was unable to confirm or reject the anecdote. In terms of pitch selection and structure, the title track is the polar opposite of a transcendental experience. It never tries to push its limits and, in fact, narrows in focus and range as the verses transition to choruses. The refrain, sung to the lines "my bella donna," sits atop two seventh chords, D minor and Eb major, which are connected at the root by a semitone. These are derived from the home key (Bb) and its relative minor (G), each casting a shadow on the other.

The start is also the end. The opening is distinguished by a traditional cadential formula of rising thirds—Eb-G, F-A, G-Bb, A-C, and Bb-D—which opens the door to a mix of resignation and resolution. The lyrics appear to be a woman's sad memories of her younger self.

Nicks insists she is still beautiful and should "come out of the darkness." However, Nicks also sings about arrogance and, through an allusion to circus tricks, something larger: don't look down so you don't fall; live bravely, eyes forward. Wachtel's guitar work features acoustic keyboard doublings, gnarled, grinding rhythmic fillers, and floating, lingering melodic fragments and echoes, which emerge as the song's standout feature. The extensive use of swells, supplemented by a volume pedal, reflects Larry Carlton's playing on Joni Mitchell's 1970s songs and contributes to the song's ambiance, as do the vocal bends and sliding framing.

Nicks' emotional reversal is astounding. Aging causes a halo to fade into a shroud, but in "Bella Donna," the halo grows brighter. The song's coda is simple, featuring Nicks and her backup singers, a piano flourish, and strummed chords. It's up close and personal.

Then there's "Leather and Lace," which Nicks wrote specifically for someone else, which is unusual for him. Waylon Jennings, the "Outlaw" country singer, balladeer, and Dukes of Hazzard narrator, commissioned it from her in 1975 for a duets album with his wife, Jessi Colter. It was returned to Nicks after Jennings and Colter divorced in 1976, citing his addictions and infidelity, as well as her "return to faith." Jennings makes no mention of the commission in his blunt memoirs, and neither does Colter in her more atmospheric account of their turbulent times together. Nicks and Don Henley recorded a demo soon after they began dating. She sings with an appealing break in her voice and plays guitar with more skill than she has ever been given credit for. Henley moves through it with grace. Another demo, from 1980, has a few incorrect starts. Sharon Celani, a singer with a dark, rich middle range, took Henley's place while he worked on another project. Despite the mistakes, the demo is stunning and could have served as an anthem for women throughout history if released. In a few takes, Benmont Tench softly counts beats in the background. Nicks pauses to adjust the timing and reassures herself that the opening guitar motif will return. Her hands sweat, and she needs to dry them. Her nails catch on one of the strings, and she curses. The second-to-last take breaks down at the end of the first verse as she sings, in a voice reminiscent of Dolly Parton's best, "I am stronger than you know."

Iovine enlisted Nicks and Henley to record the duet. He recorded their voices on different days, so the finished product lacks the intimacy that distinguishes the girl-boy and girl-girl recordings. Meanwhile, Jennings and Colter reconciled, then separated before reconciling again. They released the album Leather and Lace in 1981, the same year as Bella Donna. The song with the same title is not included because it is still in the hands of its author. Nicks and Henley also split up, with no plans for a reunion, albeit on friendly terms. When Henley decided to hold an auction and concert of golden oldies to benefit the Walden Woods Project, which is "dedicated to protecting the historic woods in Massachusetts where author/philosopher Henry David Thoreau first championed the concept of land conservation," Nicks agreed to perform. She captivated the celebrity audience at Los Angeles' Wiltern Theatre with her rendition of "At Last," a 1941 song from the Great American Songbook. Bella Donna also features her sister-in-law Lori Perry Nicks (Loretta Ann Psaltis, born 1951) as a backup singer, in addition to Celani, whom Nicks ``adopted'' in 1978. Both women were born in Los Angeles County and met Nicks' musical family by chance. Celani's story is the simplest of the two. She attended Villa Cabrini Academy in Burbank before enrolling in Ulysses S. Grant High School in Van Nuys. She was born in 1957 and raised Catholic. She sang, danced, played the piano, and, inspired by jazz legend Gene Krupa's performance on "Sing, Sing, Sing," started playing the drums. In 1972, the talented all-around entertainer joined Renaissance Women, a group of "five Valley coeds" from three different schools who sang rock, R&B, and some of their own songs. Celani relocated from Southern California to Maui, where Bobby Lozoff, another California native, had turned Blue Max, a tranquil Ka'anapali Beach cafe, into a nightclub sensation, booking stars such as Elton John and Linda Ronstadt. Celani joined a band that performed at the club. In 1978, Nicks was in Hawaii, taking stock. (During her visit, she "dropped in" on George Harrison, helped him with a song, and discussed the dangers of fame.) Nick went to Bluemax for a show one night. Nicks grabbed a tambourine and joined Celani on the other microphone, impressed by her singing and possibly free-form dancing. An ecstatic crowd took photos as one or both of them performed Warren Zevon's "Poor, Poor Pitiful Me" in Ronstadt's gender-flipped version. Celani stayed in touch with Nicks while he was on Maui and arranged for her to use a piano during her tropical vacation. Nicks invited her over to record a demo, and thus began a relationship that has lasted to this day. They lived together from 1979 to 1984.

Lori Perry's Nicks grew up in the San Fernando Valley, sang in middle and high school, and then attended business college to pursue a career in music. She was a legal secretary who also produced commercial jingles. Gordon Perry (Edward Gordon Perry III), a music producer from a well-known family who collaborated with Keith Olsen in the 1970s, married her in 1979. She met Nicks briefly in 1973 and again six years later at her husband's Dallas recording studio, Goodnight Audio, which is located in a former Baptist church. On July 23, 1978, while in Dallas for the Rumours tour, Nicks scheduled a studio session to work on the songs "Beauty and the Beast" and "Sara." Nicks first asked Perry to sing with her before signing her to perform on her solo albums, which were released between 1981 (Bella Donna) and 2001 (Trouble in Shangri-La). She possesses exceptional range, pitch, and force, as well as remarkable composure. Lori, like Sharon, accompanied Nicks on several tours and appeared with her on Saturday Night Live in 1983, which was a career highlight. She married Nicks' brother, Christopher, after she divorced Perry in 1985. Christopher did design and marketing work for his sister. The couple had a daughter, Jessica, and lived in the Phoenix neighbourhood of Paradise Valley on an estate Nicks built in 1981, close to her parents' home. Nicks sold it for $3 million in 2006. Sharon and Lori are both proud of their long-term friendship with Nicks, and they never criticise any aspect of their lives or work together. That hasn't stopped creative "fans" from creating a bogus online blog for Perry Nicks—and other Fleetwood Mac members—that turns her life in Paradise Valley into hell, focusing on her divorce from Christopher after twenty years of marriage and his serious health issues (addiction and bladder cancer). The odiousness is part of the job; Nicks ignores it, as do her backup vocalists, the "renaissance women" who drew the attention of Bella Donna reviewers—both the album and the tour that followed: "Nicks, aided by Sharon Celani and Lori Perry, creates a female vocal extravaganza with a touch of 1960s 'woo woo' soul feel."

Nicks' new label and management propelled Bella Donna to platinum status within three months. Doug Morris, the all-powerful CEO of Atlantic Records, which distributes Modern Records, propelled it to the top of the Billboard chart. Technically, Foreigner's and Journey's new albums outsold Bella Donna, but Morris wasn't concerned with the details. He contacted Willis (Bill) Wardlow, the infamous and highly corrupted Billboard chart director from 1974 to 1983, and negotiated a "quid pro quo." Nicks was invited to supper with Wardlow in order to accommodate him. She did it. Bella Donna was ranked third for a week before rising to first place.

Buckingham responded in November 1981 with his own solo album, Law and Order, which only had one hit ("Trouble") compared to Nicks' four: "Stop Draggin' My Heart Around," "Leather and Lace," "Edge of Seventeen," and "After the Glitter Fades." Meanwhile, Fleetwood travelled to Accra, Ghana, dressed in colonial attire, to record The Visitor, which briefly charted in the United States, peaking at number forty-three in 1981. The fifth track, "Don't Be Sorry, Just Be Happy," reflects the album's overall affability and apparent lack of cultural understanding. It includes Peter Green, George Harrison, drummer Lord Tiki, the Accra Roman Catholic Choir, Superbrains (a disbanded Ghanaian musical group), and the Adjo Group. It does not cohere because it does not wish to. Christine McVie also embarked on a solo trip following Tusk. Her gentle, mildly synthesised Rumours-style song "Got a Hold on Me," from her self-titled 1984 album, performed well in the United Kingdom. John McVie left Fleetwood Mac to join his former band, John Mayall & the Bluesbreakers, on tour. The Bella Donna (White Winged Dove) tour lasted only ten days, from November 28 to December 13, 1981, with five shows at the Wilshire Fox Theater in Los Angeles, followed by four songs for an all-star "Peace Sunday Committee" benefit at the Rose Bowl in front of a large audience. She wanted to continue touring, but Fleetwood Mac drew her back into the studio. The band was contractually obligated to complete work on compositions that had begun recording in September. Mick Fleetwood was already a resident of the tax haven of Monte Carlo, having bought an apartment there to avoid the Internal Revenue Service seizing his assets. Insisting that the new album not be produced in the United States, he booked the band into Château d'Hérouville, Val d'Oise, a historic residence and studio northwest of Paris. The château was constructed on the ruins of a castle in the eighteenth century, atop the graves of lords and women. The region's tourist brochures are brimming with tales of abandoned maidens, illegitimate children, secret trysts, and ghosts. The grounds had previously included an antique drinking trough, stables, a twisted garden, and a tennis court. A hall and staircase, a grand piano, and bohemian bric-a-brac separated thirty apartments into two wings on the inside. Between 1969 and 1985, the château was a popular destination for seclusion-seeking pop and rock artists, thanks to its purchase by film composer Michel Magne in 1962. David Bowie, the Bee Gees, the Grateful Dead, and Elton John have all made albums there. Jerry Garcia took acid and believed he saw Frédéric Chopin's ghost. Despite the fact that Chopin did not die at the château (he is said to have had trysts with George Sand there), Garcia held a séance in the hopes of having his ghost join his band, thankfully, on keyboards. The château's dark corners did not initially frighten Nicks. She worked with Buckingham for several weeks, lining the designated "star's bedroom" with pink fabric. She galloped around the grounds on the white horse Fleetwood had purchased, her cape flowing behind her, just like the hero in Jean Cocteau's surrealist Beauty and the Beast. She adored the film and intended to write a song about it for her second solo album. She deviated from describing the Fleetwood Mac reunion in a Rolling Stone article to describe the night she encountered the "ghost of the Château." (Her story is too similar to Henry James' 1898 novella "Turn of the Screw" and its television adaptation, The Haunting of Bly Manor, to be taken seriously, but it is entertaining as intended.) She was falling asleep in her spacious bedchamber when she heard fluttering noises and felt something brush against her cheek. The light that she had just turned off came back on. She fled in horror to her helper, who repositioned her in bed. As dawn broke over the chamber, the haunting resumed. Her room's French doors shattered with such force that furniture was knocked over and her typewriter was thrown off its stand. The kitchen staff assured her that the château's ghosts were not malicious and simply wanted to meet her. "If the ghosts are friendly and willing to talk," she went on to say, "I'm available to sit down at any time." "I'd be delighted."

The château's studios were full of music. Except for imagined noises in the night, the living quarters were quiet; Fleetwood Mac musicians did not interact. Buckingham invited Harris, while Nicks invited Iovine. The artists remained financially linked to one another while maintaining the appearance of cosy togetherness in public—hence the title of the music they composed in the ancient, dark house: Mirage. The title may refer to the band's amnesia regarding the length and dates of their stay in France: "It's all a bit of a blur—a big beautiful blur," Nicks went on to say. The best guess, based on interactions with the château's current owners and the musicians' scattered memories, is a two-month stay from December 1981 to January 1982, followed by an undetermined return in May 1982. Additional recording and engineering were done in Los Angeles before the release on June 18, 1982. Brian Wilson and others attended the listening party at Studio Instrument Rentals on Sunset Boulevard that night.

"Buckingham tossed off his songs in under two months," Pitchfork's Laura Snapes wrote about the band's quick work. "'What can I say this time?/What card should I play?' On 'Straight Back,' Nicks sings like a woman looking for inspiration. "She pulls out her well-worn tarot deck—wolf, dream, wind, sun—and whips up an unconvincing sandstorm about how 'the dream was never over, the dream has just begun,' while Fleetwood Mac became an inescapable nightmare." Perhaps, but the band had a task to complete and did so admirably, as evidenced by Snapes' subsequent comment about the album's "desperation." Nobody was killed, and no spirits were recruited.

In addition to "Straight Back," a song that is half programmatic (about Fleetwood Mac attempting to resurrect itself) and half autobiographical (about her breakup with Iovine), Nicks brought to the château a demo from the unfinished Buckingham Nicks sequel, "Designs of Love" (alternately, "That's Alright"). It dates from 1973-1974 and focuses on Nicks' "country" or "Appalachian" influences. The folk movement of the 1950s and 1960s explicitly referenced older hillbilly and blues recordings, and as these styles became commercially available, performers who had never heard them in their original form began to imitate them. Nicks' grandfather most likely knew this music before it became popular, and he preferred a more traditional style of mountain music. The pentatonic scale, which is typically (but not always) associated with both genres, is used for the stanza in "Designs of Love" to evoke mountain music and blues. Nicks sings with a country twang, channelling Jimmy Rodgers' "high lonesome" sound and the Carter Family's timbres. Buckingham's electric guitar is mixed in such a way that it sounds like a three-finger banjo, and the rhythm is typical of country and Appalachian music. His playing is clearly influenced by the Kingston Trio (commercial) style. (A different demo of "Designs of Love," on the other hand, has a sixties pop-rock groove rather than a country feel, and the version heard on Mirage is even more distant.)50 The song is in ABC form, with no rhyme scheme, and the chorus is in AABB imperfect A, rather than the ABAB or AABB used in Appalachian ballads and bluegrass songs.

Nicks wrote "Gypsy," a song about their high school days and what they promised to be for each other, for her friend Robin Snyder, who died of leukaemia. Buckingham reduced the time in the studio from 5:30 to 4:24. It was one of the album's two big singles, the other being Christine McVie and Robbie Patton's "Hold Me," and Buckingham was irritated that, once again, the hook and sentiment that resonated with the public came from his presumably less-talented former partner. The words of "Gypsy" describe a room filled with lace and paper flowers, as well as the child who remains within her, but that child, that gypsy, is dancing away, like an unfulfilled hope. Nicks refers to the Roma people, who are subjected to extravagant caricature and alternately admired (in art) and despised (in life) for their "uncivilised" independence. The song's Roma appropriation falls under the category of "angels with dirty faces" (from unknown locations). When Nicks sings about her friend's free spirit, which she shares with her own, and its loss, she invokes Carmen and other femme fatales. She refers to the Velvet Underground, which she describes as "a specific hole-in-the-wall store in San Francisco where one of Nicks' artistic influences, Janis Joplin, found most of her unique clothing." She also reminds us that she is the prima donna of her company, advancing, swaying her hips, widening her mantilla, tapping her morocco shoes, planting her fist on the hip, proud to be viewed as an exotic Other if that suits your fancy. What distinguishes a rock band's tour from global travel? The meandering demo of "Gypsy" was compressed into a shorter, more conventional form, as is customary for Fleetwood Mac. Nicks' habanera, on the other hand, retains the calm, casual playfulness of the rough takes, whereas the remix's backbeat is bouncier.

The videos weren't lighthearted. "Hold Me" was filmed in the scorching Mojave Desert. Despite being inspired by René Magritte's 1926 surrealist painting The Catapult of Desert and echoing other iconic Magritte images, the video has no explicit connection to the song, with the exception of a shot of two hands gripping near the end. Magritte depicted the unexpected and fragmented experiences that consciousness rejects but the unconscious and imagination allow back in. Surrealism is defined as a discrepancy between what one sees and what one believes they see. The film shows the band's instruments being extracted from the sand. Portraits of the band members are painted, while mirror images of them are shattered. Buckingham is present in person, appropriately dressed for the weather, at an easel, while Nicks is a desert mirage in a ruby gown and heels, sitting on a chaise couch in the sand. He'll try to paint an image of her, then give up and leave. The video's director, Steve Barron, expressed regret for the commission and painted a bleak picture of Fleetwood Mac as "not easy to work with" and uncomfortable "in the same room for long." The producer, Simon Fields, added a profane tirade about the band's fractious nature. He, too, was unpleasant to be around; it was a bad match for all of them out in the scorching heat.

Nicks is first seen in a boudoir, then in a city during the Great Depression, then somewhere in Casablanca, and finally free in a forest in the "Gypsy" video. Film noir footage is juxtaposed with rainbow colour palettes. The crystal ball shown at the beginning represents two things: seeing beyond the present, as fortune tellers believe, and childhood memories. The feathers, dolls, and flowers from the past have been preserved, protected, and secured. However, the viewpoint is that of a male voyeur peering into the boudoir through mist or smells. The camera moves around Nicks' head as she sings to herself in the mirror while performing a split on the floor. The camera enters the room, diverting her attention, and she starts acting for it while still looking in the mirror. The setting shifts to the Great Depression, with disturbing and unexpected images.

Flash forward to see her wearing a mesh netting hat, dancing among potted palms and women in furs caressing long cigarette holders. She spins in the rain, her head tilted up (the cliché of the unrestrained feminine), and the video cuts to Nicks in the present day, travelling through a pastel pink fantasy realm.

The video was extremely expensive to produce, and its lavish MTV premiere boosted album sales. Nicks assisted Russell Mulcahy in creating his storyboard. The tense dance for the camera in the mirror, as well as the strange interweaving and collapsing of symbolic and semiotic, cinematic realism and imagination, are its greatest revelations. The singer-dancer both surrenders to and commands the gaze. At the end of the video, Nicks is joined by three younger girls on a pastel cliff. They walk together, all dressed in white, implying that the hero has persevered for decades and generations to achieve dominance.

Nicks recorded her second solo album with Iovine at the helm, aware of the first's success but unwilling to change the formula. Backstage film footage of Nicks preparing for a Rolling Stone photoshoot (for the September 3, 1981 cover story "Out There with Stevie Nicks") is available. She sings the lyrics to The Wild Heart's unfinished title track over a demo of another Buckingham song, "Can't Go Back," which is featured on Mirage. She or someone else had put on the demo while applying makeup, which resulted in an unexpected Buckingham Nicks song. She moves her hips slightly, which surprises the makeup artist, who pauses as the camera zooms in. In near-perfect harmony, one of Nicks' backup singers joins her. Nicks concludes with a sly smirk. The singing is loose and carefree, much like Changing Times sounded at Arcadia High School decades ago. It's a far cry from how "Can't Go Back" and "The Wild Heart" sound on record. According to YouTube comments, Nicks' humble, natural, makeup-session singing is more popular among her fans these days than the hyperproduction associated with Iovine's collaboration with her in the early 1980s.

Sandy Stewart, a San Francisco-born, Houston-raised singer, served as Wild Heart's muse, contributing to three songs: the pounding "Nothing Ever Changes"; the new wave "If Anyone Falls," which is based on a Stewart synthesiser track called "The Last American";

and "Nightbird," a memento mori with a steady pulse, elegant arabesque of a tune, and imitative counterpoint in the chorus. The strains of "Dreams" are concealed beneath the drum machine and offbeat block chords on the keyboard, but the music is essentially its own. The bridge to the final chorus begins with a piano cascade, birdlike sounds, and the harmonised phrase "just like the white-winged dove," which pays tribute to Bella Donna.

Stewart was a friend of a friend who met Nicks in Dallas, where two tracks from Wild Heart were recorded at Goodnight Audio. She was a member of the band Sirens, which performed in smaller clubs in Texas and Louisiana. Nicks recognized Stewart's compositional contributions by singing on Cat Dancer, an edgy piano- and synth-driven album released in 1984. Unfortunately, their song "Saddest Victory" was just that (MTV aired the mopey, Billy Idol-style video, but it did not chart). Stewart became well-known as a plugger and duet performer with Nicks.

The remaining tracks blend rock, country, and disco, paying homage to Janis Joplin and Barbara Mandrell while heating up the dance floor. The album's biggest hit, "Stand Back," features Prince on keyboard. It's a foot-stomping standout from Nicks' solo repertoire, more addictive and edgier than anything on Bella Donna. Prince's involvement was a combination of chance and kismet. Nicks heard "Little Red Corvette" on the radio shortly after her wedding. While travelling to Santa Barbara for their honeymoon, she and Kim Anderson interpreted the chorus as an imperative: "Stand back." She concluded the story in front of the audience. Nicks asked Anderson, who worked for Warner Brothers, about Prince and "Corvette"; had him look in the car's glove compartment for a pen and paper so she could write lyrics; ducked into a pharmacy for cassette tapes and a boom box; and stayed up all night—ostensibly the start of her honeymoon—ping-ponging "from cassette to cassette to cassette to cassette to cassette to cassette to cassette" until her version of the song replaced Prince's original. Having the demo in hand, Iovine approached Prince on her behalf. He was based in Minneapolis and recorded in Los Angeles. "I know half of it is yours," she told Prince over the phone. "And what are you doing later?" Because we're at Sunset Sound [they were previously at A&M Studios]... "Would you like to come down and listen to it?" Prince and his bodyguard went to A&M, where he added bass and piano sections using a Roland Jupiter-8 and an Oberheim OB-X synthesiser. Because Nicks and Iovine were unfamiliar with drum machines, Prince provided percussion. "He takes an hour; he gives me a little 'I don't really know you' hug, and he's gone." "Like a tiny spirit." It's a charming image that should be added to the Fairy Investigation Society's list of sightings. Prince walked away with half of Nick's royalty.

The harmonic structure of the verses is similar in both songs: G, A, b, and G in Nicks' example, versus Bb, Ab, bb, followed by an enhanced extension (bb7, Gb7, and Gb). The progression at the start is identical, but shifted by a semitone. Although the chords for the two choruses differ (Nicks uses G, A, b, and B; Prince uses Gb, Ab, Db, Gb, Ab, and Bbm7), "Stand Back" can be sung to the tune of "Little Red Corvette" and vice versa. Likewise, the two songs' messages and meanings are similar. Prince's song, which compares a lady he can't control to a sports car, had a sensual, provocative side as well as references to prophylactics, horse racing, and one-night stands.68 Nicks prefers paradox over subversion: she tells the man who has left the room to leave; she turns away from the person she begs not to turn away; and she equates standing back with standing in line. "Corvette" is a dystopian post-disco, post-Top 40 tune that is nearly danceable (though not in platform heels), flirts with polymeter in the overdubs, and is eager to get away from its own hook because Prince has other melodic ideas he wants to try out. Nicks holds her breath and follows the rules of songwriting because her subject does. Saturday night doesn't make it any better.

There are two official videos for "Stand Back," one of which Nicks refused to watch. Director Brian Grant chose a Gone with the Wind motif for the film, setting "Tara" in Beverly Hills. Despite contributing to the storyboard and allowing the song's love struggle to be allegorized as a Civil War scene, she thought the final product was "insane—it didn't go with the song at all." "It was almost as bad as it was good." She rides a white horse toward a large white mansion dressed in an emerald-green velvet gown. The props include farm birds, a quill pen, candles, and a tavern. Goldberg appears in the battle scene with a bloodied towel wrapped around his head, while Fishkin hangs out in the bar with Nicks' backing singers. Equestrian sports did not suit her on this occasion; the horse rushed toward a clump of trees, forcing her to jump to save her life. The video was expensive to make, and Azoff called her an "idiot" for ignoring Grant. She remained firm, however, and commissioned a second film choreographed by Flashdance's Jeffrey Hornaday. It takes place in a neutral nightclub and features ensemble dancing inspired by Jerome Robbins, with allusions to Michael Jackson's "Thriller." Tensions rose again, this time between Hornaday, his fiancée, and Nicks' entourage. Hornaday disputed Iovine's revisions. Following an exchange of fuck yous, Iovine slugged Hornaday in the face, knocking him out.

"Stand Back" is frequently included in her setlists, with the shawl spinning at key moments. Mick's favourite congas and Buckingham's vocal backing are featured in Fleetwood Mac performances. Nicks did it in Landover, Maryland, in 1983, while holding, spinning, and dancing with a five-year-old girl named "Elaine," whose father worked crowd control. Her electrifying performance alongside Waddy Wachtel at her Rock & Roll Hall of Fame induction in 2019 was a tribute to Prince.

Part of her grief over his death in 2016 stems from the loss of potential. Their paths only crossed; they didn't become friends. On March 15, 1983, after a Prince concert, Nicks attended the 2 a.m. after-party he organised at the Registry Hotel (now the Mall of America Grand Hotel) in Bloomington, Minnesota. She and Prince gave an impromptu performance of his signature song, "D.M.S.R." She tapped a cowbell as Prince drummed. (It is unclear whether she contributed to the other four songs performed at the 2 a.m. jam session, or what they were.) On July 16, the day after her own show at Bloomington's Met Center, Nicks visited Prince's Kiowa Trail home studio on Lake Riley. He drove her to his purple house in his Trans Am, where they tried out some songs in the live room before whisking her away to her tour plane. The day resulted in a rough draft of the unreleased song "I Know What to Say to You," which featured call-and-response singing, synthesiser, and LinnDrum. Nicks requested that Prince accompany her on tour in 1986, but he declined due to the promotion of his Parade album. Their other interactions were purely social in nature. Nicks claimed she fled the 1984 film Purple Rain after being horrified by a scene in which Prince's character hits Apollonia, a lady who informs him she is leaving to join an all-female band. For decades, a bootleg of "All Over You" has circulated on the Internet, with much debate over whether it is an authentic duet between Nicks and Prince or a forgery. Further complicating matters was Atlantic Records' unintentional inclusion of "All Over You" on the draft list of songs and demos for Nicks' 1998 retrospective box set Enchanted. Atlantic made another error on Enchanted, including incorrect mixes of four songs from Nicks' 1994 album Street Angel, which irritated her. In reality, "All Over You" is an unfinished work by David Munday, who worked on songs with Rick Nowels and Sandy Stewart, both Prince fans. In 1983, while on tour with the Eagles, Nicks became involved with guitarist and singer-songwriter Joe Walsh. He wrote the acoustic guitar intro to "Hotel California" as well as the torn-up riff to "Life in the Fast Lane." Walsh's song "Rocky Mountain Way" is well-known, and "Life's Been Good," an elegantly funny self-confessional, remained popular well into the grunge era. Without the Eagles, he had far more lows than highs, including a two-decade hiatus between two self-parodying albums that no one heard: Songs for a Dying Planet (1992) and Analog Man (2012). Don Henley dominated the 1980s with synth-pop hits like "Dirty Laundry" and Mike Campbell's "Boys of Summer," and he even appeared on an episode of Miami Vice. Walsh did not prosper, and he does not believe he did. Everything is blank. "I wish I had 1985 to 1994 back," he has said of the time he has lost.

In 1983, he gave Nicks a new key for her roller skates. "There was nothing more important than Joe Walsh—not my music, not my songs, not anything," she stated during her eulogy. Later, Nicks relegated Walsh to "friend," effectively ending the contact sport. He described her as his "soulmate" and a "refuge." The relationship began after her divorce from Anderson and shortly after the start of the Wild Heart tour in Las Vegas on May 27, 1983, with Walsh's group opening the third show in Knoxville. Nicks' tour lasted nearly six months and was limited to the United States (her only scheduled concert in Canada, on July 19 in Toronto, was cancelled to allow her to recover). A fan stole one of Nicks' bracelets during the first of her two shows at Radio City Music Hall in New York in mid-September, prompting her to warn the 6,000-strong audience against stealing.

The tour book includes photos of Nicks' parents and the horse she rode in the cancelled "Stand Back" video. Nicks dedicated the book to Sulamith Wülfing, the artist who painted the mythical creatures she saw in visions (angels, nocturnal butterflies, sirens, mist-bathed maidens, and knights). Nicks has long admired Wülfing's art, including a set of tarot cards he previously created, and her tour attire reflected this. Nicks' jewellery, winged heart gold rings and pendants by Henri David of Philadelphia, was praised for turning "rocks and metals into aphrodisiacs." Her soft appearance did not appeal to Stephen Holden. He saw a play and sarcastically referred to Nicks as a "anachronism" for avoiding synthesisers "and a tougher post-punk stance," despite previously praising Wild Heart as a "recapitulation and broadening" of her "musical scope." The Philadelphia Inquirer was more concerned with Nicks' ability to entertain an audience than with changing tastes. "In her wispy gowns and fluttery, flyaway dance steps she executes onstage," according to the article, "Nicks plays up the dreamy aspects of her music." Her songs feature wise, young witches, strong princes, and glowering monsters—this is fairy-tale rock 'n' roll with boiling melodrama."

During the tour, she and another creature, the carefree Walsh, had plenty of time to spend together. During their "wacky years," they both admitted to playing with fire, exacerbating each other's madness. "We were on our way to hell as a couple." "It took me a long time to get over it," Nicks admitted after the flame was extinguished. Walsh had come to rely on Nicks' talent and invited her to contribute to his 1985 album Confessor. "She rode shotgun with me on that one and gave me some pointers, and she's an amazing songwriter." "If I'm left to my own devices, I'll have 85 pieces of paper with a few words on each, and folks like her and my wife, Marjorie, will now help me get 85 words on one piece of paper." There was no talk of a long-term romance, let alone marriage; they both understood that their time together would end on the road, "as rock 'n' roll relationships do." In 1988, Walsh began meeting and abusing Kristin Casey, a Texas-born stripper (she doesn't mind using that term) who later became a writer and sexual psychotherapist. The theme of a novel titled Rock Monster is her rollercoaster ride with him and the years she spent prancing around in Lucite platform heels—narcotics, booze, and BDSM included. She claims Walsh gave her three pieces from Nicks' pricey performance outfit shortly after meeting him, including "a breathtaking vintage [flapper] blouse of sheer black silk with intricate beadwork," "an antique lace peasant dress," and "a brown knit tunic with gold-and-orange detail." Casey asked why Nicks had given him her clothes. He sort of "shrugged." When I asked Casey if she still owned the three items, she showed me photos of herself wearing them. Casey also generously donated a photo of Walsh and Nicks hugging in 1991. His hand is pressed against her shoulder like Ralph's talons, which can be seen in the background. Nicks seems uneasy.

When love fails, civility triumphs: few of Nicks' friends have been completely cut loose. Her tendency is to forgive without forgetting (Buckingham is the polar opposite). In a 1986 concert, she said of the men in her life who did nothing but were up to no good, "They are poets, and yet they are the priests of nothing."

According to Dave Stewart's account of the song, "Don't Come Around Here No More," he was a poet. It is credited to Petty, but Nicks was involved in its development from the start. On April 25, 1984, Stewart and Annie Lennox (as the Eurythmics) performed at Los Angeles' Wilshire Ebell Theatre. The post-punk duo was best known for "Sweet Dreams (Are Made of This)," a synthesised shudder, and Lennox's "performed androgyny"—her short dyed hair, conservative business outfits, ice-cold glare, lipstick, and mascara. Stewart was her straight man, a duller, more predictable artist without a distinct style of his own. He recognized people in Lennox's life who were abusive to her without thinking about the possibility of being charged as another macho rock star living it up, libido unbound. Stewart appears to have valued female musicians to the point where he could profit from their talents, and he undoubtedly saw something in Lennox that was not found in popular music. Otherwise, he might misbehave around ladies.

His memoir demonstrates this. He claims Nicks went to the Eurythmics show, introduced herself to him backstage, invited him to a party at her Bavarian-style villa in Encino, and asked him to stay the night after her breakup with Joe Walsh. Out of compassion, he exploits her: "she seemed vulnerable and fragile as I was leaving that morning." He claims that the line "Don't come around here no more" came to him spontaneously in the studio. Nicks may have shouted it at him as he was leaving, or to Walsh, who arrived unexpectedly at her house.

Stewart remembers performing with Lennox at the Wiltern Theatre on April 25, not the Wilshire, and rushing to San Francisco for a concert on April 26, less than 24 hours after his unromantic visit with Nicks at her Beverly Hills home. He also claims to have written the song on the spot using a four-track Tascam Portastudio. Stewart visited Los Angeles for three days and attended the Grammy Awards on April 28. The Eurythmics then travelled to San Francisco to perform at the Kabuki Theatre.

He returned to Los Angeles in May and showed Iovine the Portastudio recording while at his home. Iovine and Stewart delivered it to Sunset Sound in Hollywood with the intention of having Nick work on it. When Nicks and Iovine started fighting, as ex-lovers do, Iovine asked Petty for help.

There remain unanswered questions. Did she sing the first take in a strange imitation of Shakespearean English, as Stewart claims, or did she leave the studio distraught because nothing seemed to be coming out right? All that is certain is that "Don't Come Around" ended up with Petty, who turned it into a hit, compensating for the injustice of losing "Stop Draggin' My Heart Around."

Stewart, Iovine, Petty, and Nicks worked together on "Don't Come Around" in another, much more likely scenario. Marilyn Martin, a Kentucky native recruited from Walsh's 1983 touring band, and Sharon Celani, one of her backup vocalists, joined her for the recording. Nicks can be heard faintly in the background but remains uncredited. She has a vague memory of Petty writing the lyrics, including the title, and then wanting the song for himself. He convinced Iovine to let his band record it. He or Iovine informed her about the news. "Even though I was deeply hurt, I knew it was a great song and that Tom deserved to sing it," she later explained. "I told him that he sounded great singing it. I didn't mention being hurt.""I kept my emotions to myself." They also recorded a lively song called "The Apartment Song," which Petty kept for later use.

"Don't Come Around" was recorded in 1984 and released as a single in 1985. It was included on Petty's album Southern Accents. Stephanie Spruill (then a backup singer with Talking Heads) contributed cello, reggae beats, and gospel elements to the song, which took weeks to complete. It also included a garage-rock conclusion (a tribute to the Ramones). The song's melody and five-chord backbone sound like Petty's, while the Coral electric sitar, drum machine, and synthesiser sound like Stewart's. Mike Campbell, Petty's longtime bandmate, performs a psychedelic solo reminiscent of Prince. The lyrics are part "snarling, angry old man at the door yelling at kids to get off his lawn," part broken-hearted lament.

The "Don't Come Around" MTV video is a crude parody of Alice in Wonderland, with Petty playing a smirking Mad Hatter and Stewart smoking a hookah on a toadstool. The song's origin is essentially a crude parody of Nicks' personal life and drug use. (Hatters allegedly went insane in nineteenth-century England after the mercury used in hat manufacturing leaked into their brains.) Stewart's final thoughts on his time with her—"I really liked Stevie, and she seemed vulnerable and fragile when I was leaving that morning"—are abhorrent.

Nicks' father predicted she would never marry because music was so important to her, and her first marriage ended almost as quickly as it began. The other relationships—with Walsh, Iovine, Henley, and, of course, Buckingham—provide tabloid fodder and serve as the foundation for "every prime-time special about a female celebrity." As the longest revolution's unfaithful daughter and partner, she ended the relationships and broke the chains. In a recent interview with Tracy Smith on CBS, she criticised the traditional notion of a woman's happiness as marrying and having children.98 The song clips played prior to and following the brief interview bolstered the criticism. If Nicks had kept "Don't Come Around," it would have been included on her third studio album, Rock a Little, which was released on November 18, 1985. Cocaine, a major player in Nicks' career at the time, exacerbated the album's long-standing creative and logistical challenges. Some tracks were revised several times before being shelved or converted into distant replicas of their former selves; others were left unfinished; and still others were produced within tight time constraints. "Battle of the Dragon," a song inspired by Sulamith Wülfing and co-written by Nicks and Petty, was never released, nor was her cover of Warren Zevon's "Reconsider Me." By the time Rock a Little was finished, Nicks' label had spent a lot of money on studio space in Dallas, Los Angeles, and New York. To management's relief, the album was a success, with four singles, two of which were played in nightclubs.

Her singing conveys the difficulties more effectively than anything she has said in interviews. She did admit, though, that "right up until the end of Rock a Little, I was fairly horrified that everybody thought there was a bunch of stuff missing on it." "What's missing?" I wonder. In Amadeus, he asks, "What notes do you want me to take out?" "What's the problem?" They won't be able to tell you. It's the same as changing for the sake of changing, rather than doing the right thing—just to say... "I think it should do this or that," or you might say, "If you don't do this on your record, it won't make it." That hurts.

Nicks is referencing Milo Forman's 1984 film Amadeus, which is about Mozart. The film depicts Emperor Joseph II's review of Mozart's 1782 opera The Abduction from the Seraglio: "Too many notes, dear Mozart, too many notes," the emperor reportedly warned the composer. "Just as many as necessary, Your Majesty," Mozart replied. Iovine or another producer suggested Nicks shorten and tighten her tracks. She claimed that the album had "a bunch of stuff missing on it." Eventually, an uneasy compromise between intense dance numbers and slower, introspective tunes with fewer layers but greater soundscapes was reached.

Iovine and Nicks' romance was over, and his enthusiasm for the project had faded. He began work on the album at Goodnight Audio in Dallas before leaving for six months. Meanwhile, Nicks had grown fond of Dallas and invested in Starck, a converted warehouse turned nightclub named after the industrial modern Parisian designer, Philippe Starck. As part of the ecstasy-fueled, pre-AIDS licentious rave phenomenon, it drew a diverse crowd, including petroleum executives, gay men, and celebrities. Girls who impressed the bouncers could skip the line. On the club's first night, May 12, 1984, Nicks and disco diva Grace Jones, one of the club's founders, performed opposite one another. The scenario provided inspiration for Rock a Little.

At Iovine's recommendation, Nicks recorded Bruce Springsteen's "Janey, Don't You Lose Heart" at Goodnight Audio. Springsteen had given her final approval for the release. She changed the chorus in the studio to the gender-neutral "Baby, don't you lose heart," which Springsteen turned down. Nicks returned the tapes to him, and the song was forgotten. She also recorded the title song and the fifth track at Goodnight Audio, both of which have long backstories. In 1981, "Rock a Little" was demoed, and "Imperial Hotel" was changed. Because two Heartbreakers—Mike Campbell and Benmont Tench—play on it, the result sounds like Tom Petty and the Heartbreakers without Petty.

In Iovine's absence, Nicks collaborated with two other producers in Los Angeles. Keith Olsen, a long-time friend of hers, joined in the spring of 1984 to produce the penultimate song, "No Spoken Word," as well as help write some of the other tracks. Rick Nowels, Iovine's assistant, also contributed to the album. Nicks expressed his displeasure with "Iovine dump[ing] me and the record into Rick's lap and sa[ying], 'Goodbye, good luck.'"

Nowels, a Palo Alto native, met Nicks at San Jose State via Robin Snyder. He and Nowels' best friend, Robin's brother Scott, formed a duo to perform in San Francisco bars, singing in two-part harmony like Simon and Garfunkel. Nicks and Buckingham walked around the house, their music blaring. Nowels was blown away by Buckingham's fingerpicking and remembers Nicks working on "Crystal" to "folk chords" on her Goya guitar. He admired her "self-assured, direct way of communicating," despite the fact that she was "just a kid" (aged twenty). Nowels and Snyder improved enough to perform set breaks for Fritz. Nowels lost contact with Nicks and Buckingham after the band split up. Snyder had a disastrous LSD trip and became one of the "Jesus freaks," destroying his career as a composer of music for anything other than the gospel.

Nowels moved to Los Angeles in 1984 after dropping out of UC Berkeley. It was too late to form a band—the people he tried to recruit all had genuine adult commitments—so "I Can't Wait," a song he'd started in a rented studio, languished. He managed to contact

Nicks' personal assistant, Glen Parrish, and admitted, "I'd love to say hello to Stevie." Parrish invited him to her home. He carried a cassette with him that contained the backing track for "I Can't Wait." He describes her as a chronic night owl, and her manager, Howard Kaufman, stayed with her until one a.m. Nowels lingered through the night, "delighted to see her" after all these years. "I lost Scott, and she had lost Robin," he said, adding that "she acted like a big sister" to him. The sun rose, and the birds began to sing. Nicks inquired about his music, and he played "I Can't Wait." She listened to the cassette several times before asking him to leave it with her. The next day, Parrish called Nowels and told him, "Stevie has written a track." You should document it." Nowels scheduled a studio session, eager to hear what she had done with the songs on the cassette. Nicks walked up to the microphone and sang, "Yes, I know you... To be continued... Nowels had a chorus for the song, which Nicks recorded, and he asked her backup vocalists to "build a wall." The next day, Iovine called and said, "It's pretty good; you guys should finish it." Nowels rescheduled the studio. The song's B part lacked words, but Nicks brought her lyric book with her, and they discovered something that connected the dots.

Her singing captures the difficulties better than anything she has said in interviews, but she did admit that "right up until the end of Rock a Little, I was fairly horrified that everybody thought there was a bunch of stuff missing on it." What's missing?" I wonder, like when he says in Amadeus, "What notes do you want me to take out?"" "What is the problem?" They won't be able to tell you. It's the same as changing for the sake of changing, not for the sake of doing the right thing—just for the sake of their stating... "I think it should do this or you should do that," or you may say, "If you don't do this on your record, it won't make it." That hurts.

Nicks is referring to Milo Forman's 1984 film Amadeus, which is about Mozart. The film shows Emperor Joseph II's review of Mozart's 1782 opera The Abduction from the Seraglio: "Too many notes, dear Mozart, too many notes," the composer was allegedly warned by the emperor. "Just as many as necessary, Your Majesty," Mozart replied. Nicks claimed that the album had "a bunch of stuff missing on it."

Iovine and Nicks' romance had ended, and his enthusiasm for the project had waned. He began work on the album at Goodnight Audio in Dallas, then left for six months. Meanwhile, Nicks had become fond of Dallas and had invested in Starck, a converted warehouse turned nightclub named after its industrial modern Parisian designer, Philippe Starck. As part of the ecstasy-fueled, pre-AIDS licentious rave phenomenon, it drew a wide audience, including

At the recommendation of Iovine, Nicks recorded Bruce Springsteen's "Janey, Don't You Lose Heart" at Goodnight Audio. Springsteen had given her final OK for its release. She modified the chorus in the studio to the gender-neutral "Baby, don't you lose heart," which Springsteen rejected. Nicks returned the tapes to him, and the song was forgotten. She also recorded the title tune and the fifth track at Goodnight Audio, both of which have lengthy backstories. In 1981, "Rock a Little" was first demoed, and "Imperial Hotel" was altered. Because two Heartbreakers—Mike Campbell and Benmont Tench—play on it, the outcome sounds like Tom Petty and the Heartbreakers without Petty.

In Iovine's absence, Nicks worked with two other producers in Los Angeles: Keith Olsen, a long-time friend of hers, came on board in the spring of 1984 to produce the penultimate song, "No Spoken Word," as well as help write some of the other tracks, and Rick Nowels, Iovine's assistant, also contributed to the record. Nicks was upset with "Iovine dump[ing] me and the record into Rick's lap and sa[ying], 'Goodbye, good luck.'"

Nowels, a Palo Alto native, met Nicks at San Jose State through Robin Snyder. He and Nowels' best friend, Robin's brother Scott, had created a pair to perform in San Francisco bars, singing two-part harmony like Simon and Garfunkel. Nicks and Buckingham walked around the home, their music blaring. Nowels was awestruck by Buckingham's fingerpicking and recalls Nicks working on "Crystal" to "folk chords" on her Goya guitar. He admired her "self-assured, direct way of commun

Nowels relocated to Los Angeles in 1984 after dropping out of UC Berkeley. It was too late to establish a band—the folks he sought to recruit all had true adult commitments—so "I Can't Wait," a song he'd begun in a leased studio, languished. He managed to contact

Glen Parrish, Nicks' personal assistant, and admitted, "I'd love to say hi to Stevie." Parrish extended an invitation to him to her home. He carried a cassette with him that had the backing track for "I Can't Wait." He recalls her as a chronic night owl, and her manager, Howard Kaufman, stayed with her until one in the morning. Nowels lingered all night, "delighted to see her" after all these years. "I lost Scott, and she had lost Robin," he explained, adding that "she acted like a big sister" to him. The sun came up, and the birds began to sing. When Nicks asked about his music, he played "I Can't Wait." She listened to the cassette a few times before asking him to leave it with her. The following day, Parrish called Nowels and informed him that "Stevie has written a track." You should document it." Nowels scheduled a studio session, eager to hear what she had done with the songs on the cassette. Nicks approached the microphone and sang, "Yes, I know you... to be continued... it's too much." "It's all about you," she added. Nowels contributed a chorus to the song, which Nicks recorded. He asked her backup vocalists to "build a wall." The following day, Iovine called and said, "It's pretty good; you guys should finish it." Nowels rescheduled the studio session. The song's B section lacked words, but Nicks brought her lyric book along, and they discovered something that connected the dots.

Her singing conveys the difficulties more effectively than anything she has said in interviews. She did admit, though, that "right up until the end of Rock a Little, I was fairly horrified that everybody thought there was a bunch of stuff missing on it." "What's missing?" I wonder. In Amadeus, he asks, "What notes do you want me to take out?" "What's the problem?" They won't be able to tell you. It's the same as changing for the sake of changing, rather than doing the right thing—just to say... "I think it should do this or that," or you might say, "If you don't do this on your record, it won't make it." That hurts.

Nicks is referencing Milo Forman's 1984 film Amadeus, which is about Mozart. The film depicts Emperor Joseph II's review of Mozart's 1782 opera The Abduction from the Seraglio: "Too many notes, dear Mozart, too many notes," the emperor reportedly warned the composer. "Just as many as necessary, Your Majesty," Mozart replied. Iovine or another producer suggested Nicks shorten and tighten her tracks. She claimed that the album had "a bunch of stuff missing on it." Eventually, an uneasy compromise between intense dance numbers and slower, introspective tunes with fewer layers but greater soundscapes was reached.

Iovine and Nicks' romance was over, and his enthusiasm for the project had faded. He began work on the album at Goodnight Audio in Dallas before leaving for six months. Meanwhile, Nicks had grown fond of Dallas and invested in Starck, a converted warehouse turned nightclub named after the industrial modern Parisian designer, Philippe Starck. As part of the ecstasy-fueled, pre-AIDS licentious rave phenomenon, it drew a diverse crowd, including petroleum executives, gay men, and celebrities. Girls who impressed the bouncers could skip the line. On the club's first night, May 12, 1984, Nicks and disco diva Grace Jones, one of the club's founders, performed opposite one another. The scenario provided inspiration for Rock a Little.

At Iovine's recommendation, Nicks recorded Bruce Springsteen's "Janey, Don't You Lose Heart" at Goodnight Audio. Springsteen had given her final approval for the release. She changed the chorus in the studio to the gender-neutral "Baby, don't you lose heart," which Springsteen turned down. Nicks returned the tapes to him, and the song was forgotten. She also recorded the title song and the fifth track at Goodnight Audio, both of which have long backstories. In 1981, "Rock a Little" was demoed, and "Imperial Hotel" was changed. Because two Heartbreakers—Mike Campbell and Benmont Tench—play on it, the result sounds like Tom Petty and the Heartbreakers without Petty.

In Iovine's absence, Nicks collaborated with two other producers in Los Angeles. Keith Olsen, a long-time friend of hers, joined in the spring of 1984 to produce the penultimate song, "No Spoken Word," as well as help write some of the other tracks. Rick Nowels, Iovine's assistant, also contributed to the album. Nicks expressed his displeasure with "Iovine dump[ing] me and the record into Rick's lap and sa[ying], 'Goodbye, good luck.'"

Nowels, a Palo Alto native, met Nicks at San Jose State via Robin Snyder. He and Nowels' best friend, Robin's brother Scott, formed a duo to perform in San Francisco bars, singing in two-part harmony like Simon and Garfunkel. Nicks and Buckingham walked around the house, their music blaring. Nowels was blown away by Buckingham's fingerpicking and remembers Nicks working on "Crystal" to "folk chords" on her Goya guitar. He admired her "self-assured, direct way of communicating," despite the fact that she was "just a kid" (aged twenty). Nowels and Snyder improved enough to perform set breaks for Fritz. Nowels lost contact with Nicks and Buckingham after the band split up. Snyder had a disastrous LSD trip and became one of the "Jesus freaks," destroying his career as a composer of music for anything other than the gospel.

Nowels moved to Los Angeles in 1984 after dropping out of UC Berkeley. It was too late to form a band—the people he tried to recruit all had genuine adult commitments—so "I Can't Wait," a song he'd started in a rented studio, languished. He managed to contact Nicks' personal assistant, Glen Parrish, and admitted, "I'd love to say hello to Stevie." Parrish invited him to her home. He carried a cassette with him that contained the backing track for "I Can't Wait." He describes her as a chronic night owl, and her manager, Howard Kaufman, stayed with her until one a.m. Nowels lingered through the night, "delighted to see her" after all these years. "I lost Scott, and she had lost Robin," he said, adding that "she acted like a big sister" to him. The sun rose, and the birds began to sing. Nicks inquired about his music, and he played "I Can't Wait." She listened to the cassette several times before asking him to leave it with her. The next day, Parrish called Nowels and told him, "Stevie has written a track." You should document it." Nowels scheduled a studio session, eager to hear what she had done with the songs on the cassette. Nicks walked up to the microphone and sang, "Yes, I know you... To be continued... Nowels had a chorus for the song, which Nicks recorded, and he asked her backup vocalists to "build a wall." The next day, Iovine called and said, "It's pretty good; you guys should finish it." Nowels rescheduled the studio. The song's B part lacked words, but Nicks brought her lyric book with her, and they discovered something that connected the dots.

Her singing captures the difficulties better than anything she has said in interviews, but she did admit that "right up until the end of Rock a Little, I was fairly horrified that everybody thought there was a bunch of stuff missing on it." What's missing?" I wonder, like when he says in Amadeus, "What notes do you want me to take out?""

"What is the problem?" They won't be able to tell you. It's the same as changing for the sake of changing, not for the sake of doing the right thing—just for the sake of their stating... "I think it should do this or you should do that," or you may say, "If you don't do this on your record, it won't make it." That hurts.

Nicks is referring to Milo Forman's 1984 film Amadeus, which is about Mozart. The film shows Emperor Joseph II's review of Mozart's 1782 opera The Abduction from the Seraglio: "Too many notes, dear Mozart, too many notes," the composer was allegedly warned by the emperor. "Just as many as necessary, Your Majesty," Mozart replied. Nicks claimed that the album had "a bunch of stuff missing on it."

Iovine and Nicks' romance had ended, and his enthusiasm for the project had waned. He began work on the album at Goodnight Audio in Dallas, then left for six months. Meanwhile, Nicks had become fond of Dallas and had invested in Starck, a converted warehouse turned nightclub named after its industrial modern Parisian designer, Philippe Starck. As part of the ecstasy-fueled, pre-AIDS licentious rave phenomenon, it drew a wide audience, including

At the recommendation of Iovine, Nicks recorded Bruce Springsteen's "Janey, Don't You Lose Heart" at Goodnight Audio. Springsteen had given her final OK for its release. She modified the chorus in the studio to the gender-neutral "Baby, don't you lose heart," which Springsteen rejected. Nicks returned the tapes to him, and the song was forgotten. She also recorded the title tune and the fifth track at Goodnight Audio, both of which have lengthy backstories. In 1981, "Rock a Little" was first demoed, and "Imperial Hotel" was altered. Because two Heartbreakers—Mike Campbell and Benmont Tench—play on it, the outcome sounds like Tom Petty and the Heartbreakers without Petty.

In Iovine's absence, Nicks worked with two other producers in Los Angeles: Keith Olsen, a long-time friend of hers, came on board in the spring of 1984 to produce the penultimate song, "No Spoken Word," as well as help write some of the other tracks, and Rick Nowels, Iovine's assistant, also contributed to the record. Nicks was upset with "Iovine dump[ing] me and the record into Rick's lap and sa[ying], 'Goodbye, good luck.'"

Nowels, a Palo Alto native, met Nicks at San Jose State through Robin Snyder. He and Nowels' best friend, Robin's brother Scott, had created a pair to perform in San Francisco bars, singing two-part harmony like Simon and Garfunkel. Nicks and Buckingham walked around the home, their music blaring. Nowels was awestruck by Buckingham's fingerpicking and recalls Nicks working on "Crystal" to "folk chords" on her Goya guitar. He admired her "self-assured, direct way of commun

Nowels relocated to Los Angeles in 1984 after dropping out of UC Berkeley. It was too late to establish a band—the folks he sought to recruit all had true adult commitments—so "I Can't Wait," a song he'd begun in a leased studio, languished. He managed to contact Glen Parrish, Nicks' personal assistant, and admitted, "I'd love to say hi to Stevie." Parrish extended an invitation to him to her home. He carried a cassette with him that had the backing track for "I Can't Wait." He recalls her as a chronic night owl, and her manager, Howard Kaufman, stayed with her until one in the morning. Nowels lingered all night, "delighted to see her" after all these years. "I lost Scott, and she had lost Robin," he explained, adding that "she acted like a big sister" to him. The sun came up, and the birds began to sing. When Nicks asked about his music, he played "I Can't Wait." She listened to the cassette a few times before asking him to leave it with her. The following day, Parrish called Nowels and informed him that "Stevie has written a track." You should document it." Nowels scheduled a studio session, eager to hear what she had done with the songs on the cassette. Nicks approached the microphone and sang, "Yes, I know you... to be continued... it's too much." "It's all about you," she added. Nowels contributed a chorus to the song, which Nicks recorded. He asked her backup vocalists to "build a wall." The following day, Iovine called and said, "It's pretty good; you guys should finish it." Nowels rescheduled the studio session. The song's B section lacked words, but Nicks brought her lyric book along, and they discovered something that connected the dots.

Iovine "saw that I was a talented guy," Nowels said. "Stevie was doing the all-night thing, and Iovine wanted to go home at midnight." He also has a long list of engagements with other musicians. Iovine went on to say, "sort of let me in to wrap it up." It was a great luxury, Nowels concluded, to have the album "dumped in his lap," because it provided him with a career. Nowels would produce the majority of the tracks, with Mick Guzauski serving as mixer.

Iovine returned to the project in 1985 and completed it at New York's Power Station studio, where he was living at the time. Nowels was still involved. Iovine worked from a hotel room a few blocks away, deciding what to keep and what to discard, as well as assembling the lineups for the final stage of recording. Iovine hired the crème de la crème of high-end session musicians for the songs that mattered (those with the most commercial potential), some for only a few hours. The musicians arrived and then left, performing the song they were told to play several times in a row with little interaction with Nicks or Iovine. Andy Newmark, who played drums on "Nightmare" and "If I Were You," the eighth and ninth tracks, described the experience, saying, "I only did one 6-hour evening recording session for Stevie Nicks at The Power Station." I think John Siegler played bass. We were in Studio A, a spacious first-floor area. Apart from saying hello and goodbye, I had little interaction with Nicks, with the exception of a few comments about the song we were listening to.

Iovine wasn't present during the recording session. Shelly Yakus, Jimmy's longtime right hand man, organised the session. Jimmy received a cassette tape of the evening's performances in his hotel room on Central Park South, where he had been staying for years. He repeatedly recorded the same song with various rhythm groups until he discovered a version he liked. Sure, it was costly, but he saw results.

Newmark completed his assignment without knowing whether or not his work would be included on the CD.

Unsurprisingly, these songs have an impersonal filler feel. They received less attention from Nicks than "Has Anyone Written Anything for You?", which she wrote with Olsen's assistance about Walsh's three-year-old daughter, who was killed in a car accident on her way to nursery school. Walsh took Nicks to see the silver drinking fountain in a park in Boulder, Colorado, that bears his daughter's name in memory: "To Emma Kristen, for all those who aren't big enough to get a drink." Her song is a slow 4/4 ballad that uses the same sinking harmonic pattern (transposed) as "Beauty and the Beast." Olsen enhanced the mix with ambient noises and eerie sounds. It concludes with the imprecation, "Poet priest of nothing."

According to Stephen Davis, another song, "Talk to Me," mentions Walsh in the lyric "You can set your secrets free, baby." No, it does not. Chas Sandford wrote the lyrics and music for "Talk to Me" in a radio-friendly, midtempo, midrange style that made it an ideal hit for Rock a Little. Sandford had written a stylistically similar song, "Missing You," with John Waite and Mark Leonard in 1984, which became an unexpected hit, first on regional radio and then rocketing up the charts—unbeknownst to Sandford, who had decamped to Super Bear Studios in France to record a demo tape. When he learned Iovine was looking for content for Nicks, he returned a copy of the cassette to Los Angeles. Iovine quickly lost it down the side of his car's front seat, seemingly permanently, until he slammed on the brakes to avoid colliding with another driver who had run a red light. Iovine took the cassette out from under the seat and listened to the "Talk to Me" demo. He knew it had the potential to be a success, so he called Sandford in the middle of the night and gave him a no-strings-attached offer to record it with Nicks. Sandford was taken aback and assumed one of his friends was playing a joke on him by perfectly impersonating Iovine's voice. But it was Iovine who was most excited to release the song as the first single from Rock a Little ("I Can't Wait" would be the second).

The song was almost finished. The drums were automated and would remain so; the double-tracked guitar was present, as was the final saxophone solo, which Sandford had patched together in Nice with a local bebopper. Nicks only needed to replace his vocal recordings with her own and have Celani and Perry build the chorus wall. However, the sessions at Village Studio B in Santa Monica, as well as the other locations where the album was produced, lasted several months. Meanwhile, the album's price soared, surpassing $1 million, much to the dismay of the label's management (Modern). A listening session for a group of executives travelling from New York was scheduled. Nick's vocals had not yet been added to the master. She'd done several takes in various locations, and the tapes had been shuffled to different machines for post-processing. (In mid-side processing, a shuffler takes the left and right signals and combines them into two distinct signals for processing, one of which is the sum of the left and right signals and the other the difference between them.) Walsh and Tench included guitar in one of the versions, which Sandford rejected as unidiomatic. The vocals were all over the place, and Sandford was in a rush to "fly" the best version into the mix. That version was recorded in New York a half-step lower than the others, necessitating pitch adjustment with a Publison Infernal Machine 90, which is used for pitch-shifting vocals. The tape was passed through the IM90 in phases before being placed on the master to ensure the most precise tuning possible. Sandford did the impossible and performed the reconstructed song. Doug Morris, Atlantic's CEO, liked it, as did Fishkin, Goldberg, and Iovine—until the machine started devouring the tape and the chorus vanished. The song that would eventually pay for the rest of the record was thankfully discovered on a digital machine to which it had been bounced.

Sandford fondly remembers the incident as an adventure "unlike anything else I have ever had in my life." Nicks had no idea about the high-pressure rush to complete "Talk to Me," and he still believes the final take of the vocals ended up on the album. She and Sandford remained in touch after the album was released, and she dedicated the single's video to Sandford's recently deceased brother Richard. Sandford recalls seeing her at a Halloween party at a "haunted" antebellum estate he used to rent on farmland outside Nashville. "She looked like Stevie Nicks with glitter on," he said, but the other guests assumed she was an imposter. The audience fell silent as she sat down at the piano and began to play.

Rock a Little is centred around two songs: "I Sing for the Things" and "Rock a Little (Go Ahead Lily)." The first, about things "money can't buy," went from a soft piano-vocal treatment to a brittle, highly arpeggiated, dulcimer-like arrangement. During the fadeout, synths and steel guitar converse. Nicks' singing is fragile and gruff, but it has less emotional impact than the original 1979 demo. The left hand contains the tonic, subdominant, and dominant pitches of C major, whereas the right hand contains only the tonic (syncopated). The voice hovers above D and F, avoiding the accompaniment's insistent cadential rhythm. Nicks dips E towards Eb in the highly unmelodic chorus to add poignancy. "Did the fear inside you / make you turn and run?" is recited, not sung, in a variety of rhythmic values on (mostly) D. Fear can be seen in the smallest pauses in elided words, minor pitch slips, and subtle quivers. These elements are emphasised in the audio-only demo, where her voice echoes before folding into a long silence after the words "turn and run." The song is dubbed "postfeminist," but no gender is specified. It discusses three types of devotion: selfless, distrusted, and desperate. The recorded version of "I Sing" fills in and deepens the I-IV-V triads (the sixth and seventh scale degrees appear), doubles the vocal line at the third and occasional second, and adds rhythmic complexity. It also "normalises" the song, as Matthew Hough points out in his analysis: phrase lengths, metre, and tonality are all more clearly defined. Nonetheless, Nicks' song expresses a lack of definition.

"Rock a Little (Go Ahead Lily)" is a song about her father, Jess Nicks, who once pushed her onto the stage while she was ill, using her literary alter ego, Lillian Hellman. (In her 1970s and 1980s poems, Nicks referred to herself as Lily and her best friend, Robin, as Julia, alluding to the 1977 film Julia about heroic self-sacrifice. The gentlest reggae patterns rock a little, but not significantly. The title track from her most upbeat album starts as a lullaby and progresses to a eulogy. The cradle rocks at birth, just like a rocking chair does before death. We rock from side to side as the years pass. Herbert Worthington's photographs of Nicks in black next to a black cradle and rocking chair capture the idea. Except for the furniture, the record cover was made out of these materials.

Like "I Can't Wait," "Rock a Little" required time and effort to complete. Nowels recalls finishing a rough monitor mix at 6 a.m. and presenting it to Nicks for approval. Mick Guzauski's version of "Rock a Little" was rejected, and she preferred a mix from six months prior. She returned to the studio to manually adjust the faders, producing a track that Nowels couldn't understand because "the levels were all over the place." "Do you think a 14-year-old kid thinks about that?" Nicks asked. They focus on the record's vibe." He never forgot everything he had learned. The "vibe" is hot, humid, and sultry. The phrases "funny little dancer" and "rock and roll ballerina," which her father wrote when she was a child, swirl through the heat. The backup vocalists breathe the title syllables into the mix at odd intervals, while a maraca shakes out eighths in the foreground, near the ear. The longer version, which features live drumming and new lyrics, is less monotonous and enhances the original's mild reggae flavour.

"Rock a Little" was the album's default title. The album was supposed to be called The Other Side of the Mirror, after a song in the works called "Mirror, Mirror." Nicks saved that name for later, and the song wound up as a terrible B-side to a 1994 cassette single. "I didn't like the way it came out," she said, before adding a strange footnote: "'Mirror, Mirror' is the other side of the mirror, and the Gemini personality." The two, nine, or ten personas I have, and how I manage them all." Throughout the mid-1980s, she spoke in circles, round and round, expressing the sensation of not knowing where she is while staring at herself—at herself—in a hall of mirrors. It was a terrifying emotion, and it inspired a terrifying song, which was left off the album despite showing great promise. The "Night Gallery" demo lasts two minutes, but the chorus and two verses were polished out with keyboard and tambourine, giving it a fragile intensity. Nicks switches from "I" to "she" and invites her boyfriend to accompany her "deep into the end zone of the moor, where hounds bay and witches fly brooms, and belief in the supernatural is as natural as breathing, or not breathing." Nicks' title was inspired by Rod Serling's introduction to the 1970-73 television series Night Gallery. In the second section of the series' first episode ("Eyes," directed by Steven Spielberg), Joan Crawford plays a blind woman who regains her vision during a New York City blackout. Nicks' song, as recorded on cassette, is a congested hothouse in contrast to Serling and Crawford's "cool dampness."

It's the ideal song for Rock a Little, but it wasn't finished on time and thus couldn't be included, shifting the album's emphasis away from the personal and toward more genetically upbeat music.

The sounds favoured by the renowned bands of the 1980s, such as "carousel keyboards, blocky rhythms, and splashes of controlled guitar anarchy," were diametrically opposed to Nicks's Americana, but she persuaded herself to change with the industry. Despite the era's emphasis on thrilling the senses with detached major-key melodies, she sang from the heart, with her seasoned country-rock timbre taking precedence over the notes and chords. "I Can't Wait" is a tightly wrapped dance track with a "wall" of backup vocals in the final mix, much like New Order's "The Price of Love." Nicks' vocals and demeanour remain too sharp for click tunes. Mark Coleman of Rolling Stone couldn't understand Rock a Little, saying that "for a pop album," it "sounds strangely distant, out of touch." When Stevie's saccharine moans are juxtaposed with purring synths and drum machine pattern, they sound harsh and startling. Attempts to 'contemporize' some of these 4/4 strum-along ditties spoil what would otherwise be a pure oddity, a relic from the singer/songwriter's forgotten period." Coleman would have written an ideal review if he had admitted that the record enchanted him. Nicks travelled from April 11 to August 28, 1986, starting in Houston, Texas and ending in Long Beach, California. Between September 24 and October 6, there were eight additional dates in Australia. She was ill, her voice was overworked, she experienced vertigo, and she once fell off stage. It's difficult to watch the concert film Live at Red Rocks. It was first released in 1987 as an improved CD-ROM and later reissued on DVD in 2007. The video uses close-ups, overdubbed vocals, and visual effects to conceal performance flaws. The video begins with a montage featuring the album's first song, "I Can't Wait." Mick Fleetwood, Waddy Wachtel, Peter Frampton, and Nicks are greeted by fans upon arrival at Red Rocks Amphitheatre in Morrison, Colorado. Nicks sings hoarsely into a flower-draped microphone stand on stage. During "Beauty and the Beast," images from the 1970s are intercut with the action. Fleetwood is the beast, and she is beautiful. Nicks marches across the stage in pumps, tossing her hands up as if casting a spell on the backup musicians, as the band begins their entrance to "Stand Back." A stagehand hands her a white dove, which holds the microphone. "Edge of Seventeen" runs nearly ten minutes (six minutes longer than the song), with the band riffing for three of them. Nicks is no longer the bohemian in flowing caftans; instead, she portrays a more cryptic and protective character. She walks behind Wachtel, pausing at an incredible port de bras, her wide white sleeves shaped like wings. Her performance alternates between full-throttle singing and abstract, poetic speech: "Well, when it rains, the sky never expects it, but the sea changes colour." She kneels down to the stage, hugging the microphone, and yells as if uncaged, about two-thirds of the way through.

On May 11, 1985, long before the release of Rock a Little and the tour, Nicks gave an interview in Los Angeles. She still appears twenty, but she is tall, and she speaks hazily and lyrically about an album that wasn't right until she thought about it for a "few minutes, few days, few lifetimes." She requests to use the restroom, most likely for a bump, but is unable to do so because she is already connected to a microphone. Nicks musters the courage to engage the interviewer, smiling and laughing. When she discusses being famous in a male-dominated environment, she becomes serious. She was "lucky," she claims, because she was "protected" and did not have to "see too much." Christine experienced "hard knocks" as a member of Fleetwood Mac. Nicks is clearly in pain during the interview, which is still available to watch online. The pain persisted, and the albums she released after Rock a Little were uneven for reasons specific to her as well as changes in the recording industry as a whole. Before going into the studio, she wrote songs about being dragged around physically, emotionally, and creatively and attempting to stop it. It took years for her to become free. To become a star or superstar, you need talent, timing, and the right kind of push from profiteers. To become an icon and find happiness in the afterglow, a reckoning is necessary. Finally, Nicks was able to express the pain of others through her music.

CHAPTER 6
SARA

Nicks checked into the Betty Ford Center in Rancho Mirage, California, in late November 1986, between concert tours, to treat her cocaine addiction, which she had been fighting for a dozen years (four years longer than the eight she spent in denial). She attempted to quit smoking in 1982, but gave up while filming the "Gypsy" music video. A doctor friend warned her about the damage she had caused to the inside of her nose (from cocaine and the mountain of aspirin she took for withdrawal headaches) and the risk of a fatal haemorrhage if she continued to use it. Friends and family, including her parents, encouraged her to seek help. She booked a room at Betty Ford under the name Sara Anderson. It was a brief, monotonous experience living in a dorm with a middle-aged female alcoholic, doing chores (mopping, vacuuming, and cleaning the grounds), and going to nine-to-five counselling sessions. It was far from the "boot camp" she describes. When her presence in the clinic was revealed, fans buried her (and the staff) with flowers, plants, and love letters. Following her discharge, Nicks approached Ford and thanked her on bended knee for saving her life. In 1986, she stayed at the clinic for two and a half weeks, leaving earlier than planned (the recommended stay is a month), but she remained clean.

In three songs, she alluded to her experience, albeit hazily. Nicks must have read or watched Margaret Mitchell's 1936 novel Gone with the Wind while detoxing, because "Welcome to the Room, Sara," which she gave to Fleetwood Mac to record, alludes to the melodrama's themes of love, including loving something imagined. "Sara" rhymes with "Tara," Scarlett O'Hara's plantation name, and an ancient word for stars, "soul's light." Buckingham portrays Rhett Butler, who spars with his soulmate and alter ego Scarlett. The song is also self-referential, with the line "welcome to the choir, sir" recalling the lyrics to "Silver Springs," "Beautiful Child," and "Sara." Anyone who has been in treatment can understand the line, "When you hang up the phone, you cease to exist." It also expands on Scarlett's famous line, "Wherever shall I go?"

Buckingham added programmed bongo drums to the song to help it fit in with the rest of the album, and Fleetwood created an inert recitation?The chorus is based on a single major chord, with snare and tom-tom fills. Buckingham doubles Nicks' vocals on the chorus, but in an awkward and unmusical way. It's a recurring theme throughout the album, as is the jangling guitar, which adds brightness to a song devoid of any sort of hook. The Fairlight CMI is overprescribed, and "Welcome to the Room" becomes unconscious.

"When I See You Again," which Nicks also attributed to Fleetwood Mac, is a disjointed and barely articulate song. Nicks' voice sounds scratchy and dry to the ear. The song is a country ballad with accidental off-key tuning. According to Buckingham's production, Nicks only sings a few verses and the chorus in stitched-together segments. Nylon-stringed guitar, gentle tambourine and shaker sounds, distant keyboard flutters in the chorus, and a synthesised string line round out the song's instrumentation. Suspended seconds and fourths add weight: the verses are defined by Asus2 and Esus4, and the chorus by Bsus4 and Asus2. The music conveys the sense of confusion in the second verse, which describes aimless wandering down halls and staring at stairs. Buckingham takes over as Nicks' singer in the final section, bringing the song to a close while making the effort clear to all.

"Doing the Best That I Can" came out two years after the other songs. The film's subtitle, "Escape from Berlin," refers to both the fall of the Berlin Wall and the Berlin-based film Julia (1977). The film, which examines the experience of being imprisoned, clearly spoke to Nicks. The studio musicians chosen for the song (which appears on her fourth solo album, 1989's The Other Side of the Mirror) are excellent but uncommitted, with their comings and goings as audible here as on Rock a Little four years ago. The chord changes (Eb major and minor, Bb minor, Ab major, G minor, and Bb major) are subtle, with a spooky nod to Mike Oldfield's "Tubular Bells" on the rhythm guitar. The texture blurs the verse and chorus, and the power-rock sound makes up for the flaws in the confessional lyrics, a detail that sinks the track but lifts the album.

"Rather than rock's Shirley MacLaine, this time she's more Sylvia Plath," Steve Hochman opined in the Los Angeles Times about Nicks' current phase, "though Nicks has apparently crawled out from under her unspecified bell jar." Images of brooding solitude and hard lessons learned abound: there's a lot of falling rain and disillusioned fairy-tale princesses, all sung about in an appropriately weary but wise voice." His skewed view of female artistry and suffering irritates me. Nicks rose to prominence as feminism became more mainstream; the opposition she faced was not monolithic, but rather porous enough to allow her to launch a solo career and thus be credited with contributing to the movement's success. Nicks made compromises in order to survive, and once she had risen above all of her tormentors, she was able to confidently and casually leave disillusionment behind.

From November 1985 to March 1987, Buckingham worked intermittently on the Fleetwood Mac album Tango in the Night. A month later, it was released with cover art by Brett-Livingstone Strong: his 1987 painting Homage to Henri Rousseau, which Buckingham had bought for his home. The reference is to Rousseau's

1907 novel La charmeuse des serpents. The snake charmer uses her pipe to play seductive music, causing serpents to dance in a fantastical, moonlit jungle setting. It's as seductive as a profane Garden of Eden, and Sylvia Plath wrote a poem about it titled "Snake Charmer" in 1960. Her eight stanzas veer wildly from a description of an artist's creative abilities to imaginative concepts. (Rousseau never visited India, which inspired his famous images.) The snakes represent both the charmer's audience and her creation. The artist generates something from nothing and nothing from something. The demo evolves into a song, which in turn evolves into another demo.

Nicks sent in demos for "Welcome to the Room" and "Doing the Best I Can," but due to health issues, she only stayed in the studio for two weeks. Buckingham and Dashut produced the album, which was engineered by Greg Dorman, an Ohio transplant who previously worked with Joe Walsh. He worked at Rumbo Studio in Canoga Park, which was constructed by Daryl Dragon, the husband of Captain & Tennille, a light-rock couple. The structure was a grey cement slab with two elephant statues and a blue awning above the entrance. It was active "at a time when the Valley lingered somewhere between Frank Zappa's ramblings and a real-life version of Paul Thomas Anderson's Boogie Nights," according to a LA Weekly article. "A mix of agriculture, dust, white wagon wheels, diners, car dealerships, suburban sprawl, new housing developments, and swimming pools, it was held together by all those long streets and lazy vowels." Rambo's slacker vibe made it popular in the 1980s among hair bands such as Guns N' Roses. Dorman and Dashut first met in 1986, when they were recording Christine McVie's cover of "Can't Help Falling in Love" for Blake Edwards' slapstick comedy A Fine Mess. Buckingham reserved a Rumbo studio for a solo project while simultaneously working on Tango in the Night in another studio. He, like Tusk, recorded at home in Bel Air. Mick Fleetwood and the McVies sat in an RV parked in the driveway, waiting to be transported to Buckingham's laboratory (the studio across the hall from his bedroom) for overdubbing. The work was professional and cost-effective.

Tango is a paradox, a cross between fake orgy and fake afterorgy. "There's a phenomenal wholeness to the recordings on Tango that seems like a superficial compensation for how deeply fragmented the band was at the time," Brad Nelson, a critic who writes about music, says. Certain tracks, such as "Family Man," are heavily processed blends of analog and digital sounds, whereas others, such as "Seven Wonders," are delicate structures padded with reverb. The song barely holds together, and precision keeps the tango from becoming kitsch. The ostinato grunting that serves as the hook in "Big Love" is precisely timed to the drum machine, evoking the "heavy breathing" of 1970s pop rock pornography.

Buckingham experimented as usual, listening to tracks at different speeds to fine-tune the mixes (a form of torture for the production team), as well as recording at half- and quarter-speeds to make the higher end sound richer when brought up to speed. The result is a smooth and expansive analog-digital mix, especially on the album's first three singles: "Big Love," "Seven Wonders," and "Little Lies." Each was recorded across 46 tracks. According to a Salon magazine investigation into the album's creation, Buckingham was inspired by Kate Bush's hybrid electroacoustic sound world. To avoid deterioration, digital tapes were cut, spliced, and refrigerated. Dorman would experience panic attacks whenever the fickle, prickly Buckingham changed his mind, expressed disappointment, or decided he needed to do everything himself at home.

One of the few photos from the recording sessions shows Nicks wearing thick reading glasses and a loose white skirt and sweater. Buckingham and Christine McVie are dressed similarly, and they appear to be recording vocals for "Seven Wonders." Sandy Stewart, who plays a key role on The Wild Heart album, is co-credited as a songwriter alongside Nicks. According to internet lore, which Stewart called "false and inaccurate", Nicks sang the wrong words in the studio and became a co-writer by default. The text changed, but not by chance. "All the way down you held the line" became "all the way down to Emmeline" on the demo, and "rainbow's end" became "rainbow's edge," a change similar to "age/edge of seventeen." "Seven Wonders" describes true love, or true lost love, as being greater than the pyramids and Babylonian Hanging Gardens, which is straightforward enough except for the inclusion of "Aaron" in the post-chorus. Nicks isn't talking about her grandfather here; she's experimenting with phonemes to make language more musical. The verses and chorus are framed by an intro and outro that explore

Fairlight's wonders while offering commodified exotica: eerie synth hooks, parallel fifths, a hazy, lazy beat, sponginess, and squishiness. Tango in the Night makes Rumours seem real; everything is a ruse. The B-side to the 'Seven Wonders' single is an instrumental called "Book of Miracles," which became "Juliet" on Nicks' Other Side of the Mirror album. "Ooh My Love" was also included on the solo album after being removed from Tango. Another unreleased outtake, "Joan of Arc," was reconstructed using reel tape. Its absence is felt. The song isn't finished, but it deserves to be heard with the lap harp's foreground-background echoes, eerie guitar wails in the far back of the mix, clamped tingling of the tambourine, and huskily frail singing of the line "turn it to the wall... up against the wall." It fades out inconclusively, reflecting the lyrics' obscurity. The bend bar on the electric guitar (which is used beautifully near the end of the song) may have evolved as an attempt to imitate the dobro. The otherworldly background sounds, but not the distressed singing, are evenly distributed. The lyrics are free-form (Nicks generally avoids ABAB or AABB balladry) and are linked to the first five notes of the major (or Mixolydian, minus the sixth and seventh). The attack, detail, amplitude, and colour of the obsessive repetitions "turn it to the wall... up against the wall" vary. The differences in dynamics, the unevenness, the way the notes are stretched out, sped up, enlarged, or reined in, and the flexibility in the shape and texture of the three phrases are all examples of processing. "Joan" is an enigmatic love song that combines references to ancient legends, limousines, and a personal incident. It conveys anguish while describing betrayal and bad faith. The hero is doomed as he ascends the scaffold, over the pyre, and above the flame tongues. Shooting squads are known to line up people against a wall. Hine was born on September 21, 1947, in Wimbledon, London, just eight months before taking the name of the woman he married. His father was a lumber salesman and his mother a nurse. He was interested in architecture before discovering music and teaching himself how to play the piano. Hine was a member of several bands and released several records before focusing on production as a "accomplished synth player and rhythm programmer." He told an interviewer that he "never wanted to be a rock star," instead aspiring to be an interdisciplinary artist like his first wife Natasha Barrault. (Barrault has worked as a songwriter, filmmaker, interior designer, and seamstress with sustainable materials. Hine's musical interests ranged from folk to jazz to art rock; he composed for film, produced albums, and, most recently, developed music-making apps. He loved Mahler's symphonies, the organ, and the harpsichord. Hine pioneered sound effects that became eighties clichés, only to deconstruct them in the 1990s, enraged by the industry's indifference. He wrote electronic and acoustic hits for artists such as Tina Turner, Howard Jones, Duncan Sheik, and Suzanne Vega. Then he went acoustic, recording an album for the fractious French band Les Négresses Vertes in the natural acoustics of a hotel lobby in the French Pyrenees.

Nicks met Hine at Doug Morris's suggestion, and the two worked together on her fourth studio album, The Other Side of the Mirror. Both were looking for a Beauty and the Beast setting for the project, so they chose a fake castle built in Beverly Hills in 1974. The semi-fortified pile at 1366 Angelo Drive had previously appeared in films (pornography was shot in its over-draped rooms), and Nicks' (aka Iovine's) team converted it into a functional studio. According to Davis, Nicks rented "Castle Studios" for a half-year at $25,000 per month. Nicks and Hine lived there, along with her brother's wife, Lori Perry Nicks, and Nicks' assistant, Karen Johnston. On May 18, 1989, she hosted rock gods Billy Idol and Gene Simmons, dressed in campy black leather, at the release party for The Other Side of the Mirror on the premises.

Nicks and Hine got along well, but their relationship ended abruptly in Buckinghamshire, according to her. The obvious reason is his semi-estranged wife's pregnancy. Barrault gave birth to her son in London in May 1989. The album Nicks had made with her courtly lover was released the same month, eight time zones apart. Hine did not finish the project, so Nicks hired Chris Lord-Alge, whose recording style fell somewhere between "hard hitting" and "hit-parade friendly" rock in the 1980s, which was exactly what Nicks, Modern, and Atlantic wanted. Lord-Alge finished production and engineered The Other Side in his Los Angeles studio using a Sony 3348 48-track digital machine, which was top of the line in 1989. Chris' brother Tom also contributed to the album, remixing the fourth single, "Whole Lotta Trouble," one of three songs co-written by Mike Campbell, Tom Petty's guitarist.

Hine complained back in England that he was shut out of the process and that his phone calls had not been returned. Nicks had him removed from her personal life. However, business being what it is, he was given due and generous credit for his creative and technical contributions to an album that sounded less eclectic at the end than it did at the start.

The Other Side was inspired by Lewis Carroll's Alice's Adventures in Wonderland and its sequel, Through the Looking-Glass, but it's a rather diverse offering that incorporates other children's tales, from Red Riding Hood to the entire cosmos of legends about maidens trapped (or protected) in castles. Nicks dedicated it in memory of her grandmother.

The album's lyrics, like Carroll's story, are consistently disorienting. The plural and singular merge, while the same things are made to appear different. Several songwriters are named, some of whom are strangers, while others are friends and colleagues. Nicks collaborated with Rick Nowels on two of the songs, including the single "Rooms on Fire," which is about the heat generated by her affair with Hine. "Well, maybe I'm just thinking that the rooms are all on fire," Nicks said. "Every time that you walk in the room." The first line is metrically correct, but the second is not; the words "every time" are distorted and mangled at the beginning of the phrase. The official video for this song shows Nicks briefly holding a beautiful blond baby, evoking the context of her divorce from Hine. Her character, dressed in flowing white silk, hands the child back to a man in black after presumably choosing to spend her life alone. (Nicks decided not to wear old-age makeup in the video.) The lyrics' "magic" and "fire" are mirrored in the music, with chimes and flamenco-style guitar breaks attempting to liven up the predictable chorus. Hine, Nicks, and Nowels all played on "Two Kinds of Love." Although Nicks performs it with Bruce Hornsby, a demo of Hine singing the song alone with his own lyrics circulates online, putting the song's origins with him. The produced song, which is based on Nicks' lyrics, casually mentions a third figure, a "famous friend"—namely, Petty. Through the looking glass, we see relationships within relationships.

"Cry Wolf" is by Jude Johnstone, a Celtic folk and jazz singer who describes herself as the author of "the saddest song on everyone's album." Michael Solomon, a plugger, pitched the song to Nicks, who decided to record it and invited Johnstone to the sessions. Johnstone had previously met Nicks in the late 1970s at the Sunset Marquis Hotel in Los Angeles, when Fleetwood Mac was at the pinnacle of their fame. Nicks was "effing gorgeous," she remembers, "at the pool, coked out, because, you know, none of them ever slept." By the late 1980s, Nicks was a completely different person: smarter, tougher, and wiser. Johnstone admired her brilliant wit, "the cat's [Nicks's] sharp humour," and the fact that she was past the "whole rock star thing," rolling her eyes and drawing, "oh yeah," about it all: "She's hipper than anyone knows." She and Him had something going on," Johnstone recalls, but "he didn't get how great she was' ' and made her do "Cry Wolf ' take after take without rhyme or reason. Nicks simply "laid it out" like a pro, but Hine's production "mucked it up," destroying the groove. Nicks and Johnstone got together to discuss writing a song together, but it didn't work out because it became "too precious." When asked why she decided to record "Cry Wolf," a song "about a guy who ran off," Nicks said, "because I wished I'd written it."

Tango in the Night outtakes include "Juliet" and "Ooh My Love." Nicks inadvertently stole the latter's tune from Petty's cassette tape. She assumed Mike Campbell had made the tape for her and that she was free to listen to its contents—demos that Petty had decided not to include on his next album—to see if anything piqued her interest. But she chose the wrong tape, one that contained music Petty wanted to keep rather than discard. He was enraged by the mix-up. Due to Petty's busy schedule, Hine enlisted Fixx guitarist Jamie West-Oram to play on "Ooh My Love" and several other tracks on The Other Side.

Another song, "Alice," has the unusual effect of Lewis Carroll surrealism. According to English literature scholar Michael Wood, Carroll enjoyed puns and portmanteaus, especially those that revealed the "secret life" of repressed behaviours. Carroll's satire was balanced by a serious love of the absurd, and Nicks' lyrics are similarly knowingly nonsensical but full of possible interpretations. She employs words to cast spells, enchanting people with her allusions. A "solid piece of armour" is a "steel-plated vest," but Nicks substitutes "or" for "is." The text connects seemingly disparate metaphors. Reviewers typically raise their hands in frustration as they attempt to decipher Nicks' language, perplexed by the lack of narrative threads. "Alice," on the other hand, makes sense as a reference to her grandmother Alice, a frontierswoman who read Carroll's books to her. The real Alice, not the fictional one, travelled through Mountain City in the southwest (mentioned in the first verse) and wore a garter with a stiletto heel (mentioned in the third verse).

In response to Tennyson's lament for his beloved, poet Arthur Henry Hallam, who died of a stroke at the age of twenty-two, Nicks inserts the line "Ah but it's better not to lose." It serves as a bookend to her adaptation of Edgar Allan Poe's "Annabel Lee," an 1849 poem about a bride's death. Poe wrote about doomed love elsewhere, but this text is about his own wife's death from tuberculosis. The angels are envious of the narrator's feelings for the maiden he meets in a magical seaside kingdom. He lies beside her body in her sepulchre after she dies. After reading the poem for Mr. Clements' English class, Nicks wrote "Annabel Lee" in her senior year of high school. She sang it for her mother on the guitar. The song circulated as a demo for Trouble in Shangri-La, but it wasn't recorded and released until 2011, on Nicks' album In Your Dreams, which he co-created with Dave Stewart. Nicks, like "Affairs of the Heart," kept Annabel Lee" close for decades, recording it after she had exorcised the demons of the past, the bad loves, and the toxic habits. "Garbo" is another example, but it deals with exploitation. Buckingham lurks, but not as threateningly. To quote Emily Brontë's Wuthering Heights, a gothic Romantic novel written around the same time as the Tennyson and Poe poems, she was finished playing Catherine to Heathcliff.

Because Nicks' mother, Barbara, underwent major heart surgery in the summer of 1989, he moved to the desert to be with family and recorded the vocals for Behind the Mask in Phoenix. Producer Greg Ladanyi flew in to assist and recorded a more stripped-down, spacious album than Tango in the Night—no eclecticism, no decadence (compared to Buckingham's projects), but flat sales. Following the release on April 9, 1990, the band accelerated with the two hotshot guitarists and toured extensively. The magic, however, belonged to the past, as Mick Fleetwood focused on his memoirs rather than music. During the tour, he released a tell-all autobiography (the first of two) about the band. It didn't reveal everything, and Nicks was uninterested in his memories of their long-ago romance. Following the tour, the band broke up again, with each core member blaming the others for reasons no one could recall. Nicks had forgotten the hotels, the cities, and what happened next—her recording an album that Rob Sheffield, who almost never criticises her music, described as a "tranquilised dud." Few people heard it. Street Angel was Sheffield's low point: "The benzos had taken over."

True, benzodiazepines had dominated her life, but not her art. Nicks decided to stop drinking after undergoing cocaine addiction treatment at Betty Ford in 1986. She contacted a West Hollywood psychiatrist (whose name she has not revealed) who prescribed clonazepam, which sent her into a depression. Instead of gradually weaning her off the anticonvulsant, he increased her dosage, which increased her listlessness and caused weight gain. The malpractice lasted eight years, including several albums, her mother's heart surgery, and numerous performances. "I started to notice that I was shaking all the time [a common side effect of high doses of the drug], and I'm noticing that everybody else is noticing it too," Nicks said. And then I start to wonder, "Do I have some kind of neurological disease, and am I dying?" She lived in a void and might have remained there if not for her mother's intervention and Glen Parrish, her live-in personal assistant during the worst period of her cocaine addiction (1980–1986) and later a member of her management team. He offered to take her massive daily dose of clonazepam—just once—to see how she would react. After thirty minutes, he felt numb and dizzy and was unable to drive. Nicks contacted her psychiatrist, who chastised her for disclosing her medication. "The first thing he said was, 'Are you trying to kill him?'" "And the next thing I said was, 'Are you trying to kill me?'" In 1993, she sought treatment at Daniel Freeman Marina Hospital's chemical dependency unit in Marina Del Rey. "I moulted," she explained of the abrupt discontinuation of clonazepam. "My hair turned grey." My skin started peeling completely. "I was in excruciating pain." The small, nonprofit hospital has closed its doors. It treated both high-profile patients and those who had been placed there by the legal system. It was a Catholic health provider known for combining physiological, spiritual, and psychological approaches to addiction. Nicks would have stayed for a month, the maximum time allowed, and agreed to acupuncture treatments to help her at her lowest point.

Street Angel was created both before and after this calamitous period, and it involved more than one producer. Glyn Johns started the project in 1992, and Thom Panunzio completed it. The album began with a month and a half of preparation time at home in Los Angeles. Nicks collaborated with guitarist Andy Fairweather Low, best known for his work with Eric Clapton, and guitarist Bernie Leadon, a founding member of the Eagles. The original plan was to record an album with a strong acoustic feel (Leadon played several string instruments and was well-versed in traditional country music and bluegrass), in a positive setting with incense and candles. The emphasis will be on social issues. When it came to recording the demos, Nicks didn't want to be a strict "taskmaster," she explained. The music was not as upbeat as The Other Side of the Mirror, but the approach to recording the album was initially optimistic. "I'm really excited about what's to come because I'm so not excited about what just went by," she told a reporter. Johns was hired based on his discography, not his manners. Irritable, snippy, and generally rude, he treated Nicks in the same way he treated other artists he deemed distracted or unproductive: by policing her work to the point of barring her from the studio. He had achieved enormous success with the Eagles, Rolling Stones, Led Zeppelin, and Clapton (who he referred to as "lazy") and, as a true authoritarian, could not be questioned. When he was finished, he packed his belongings and left, leaving his name off the liner notes. "I definitely knew what it was like to come up against a really strong-willed Englishman," Nicks said about their failed collaboration. "I knew it would not be easy. But I never imagined I would lose." Her dignity suffered less than the bottom line. She accepted the possibility of ruining the album and her initial enthusiasm for it.

Glyn does not mention Street Angel in his memoir, Sound Man. Panunzio delegated some of his responsibilities to his twenty-three-year-old son, Ethan, an aspiring producer who played percussion on Street Angel and presented Nicks with two songs that ended up as bonus tracks. "I was initially called in because I had written a couple of songs they wanted to record," he said, "and I went out to LA to help with those." They were not part of the final cut. I remember a few enjoyable days of pre-production with Mike Campbell at Stevie's house; we all got along well, and I ended up playing on roughly half of the record. It was an honour to meet and play alongside Benmont Tench. Ben and I became close friends after that. When I listened to the record, I was surprised by how much I contributed. I was there for only a few weeks.

"Docklands" is sung matter-of-factly until Nicks and her backup singers sing "hold on," at which point the song nearly comes to an end. The lyrics describe the dispossessed of southeast London and are similar to the lyrics of the title track, "Street Angel," sung by Nicks and David Crosby, with whom Johns previously collaborated on the flop album Thousand Roads. Because they are so close, their voices blend even better. She had previously sung with men on big hits, and that must have been the intention here—a hetero musical bonding experience—but the end result has a troubling double-edged ambiguity: the song is lonelier because it is a duet. It's about homeless kids who give up and don't care, as well as an addict's hopelessness. The impetus for its creation was usually spontaneous. Nicks was forced to relocate to the Peninsula Hotel in Los Angeles after her home became infested with bees. "We had to go," she went on to explain, "'cause the bees were so intense that they had to be moved, not killed, but moved." In her hotel room, she watched a couple of homelessness movies on television, which inspired a song about a wastrel who is given the chance to escape the streets through romance but is unable to do so.

The LinnDrum pattern is similar to Phil Collins' "In the Air Tonight," but lacks the explosive release of that song. Nicks mentions Charles Dickens, whose fiction highlighted the plight of street angels. It's a departure from the song's autobiographical themes. "I fell down the stairs a broken rag doll," the scariest and most tired line, is performed throughout Street Angel, the bereaved, besieged artist's most disconnected, disarticulated album. Her handlers wanted it to happen because their livelihoods depended on her. She willed herself to resist the producer, but eventually gave up on the project.

Her angels looked after her in the studio and during the low-budget road trip. She travelled with a group of friends. Sara Recor (aka Sara

Fleetwood), Sharon Celani, and Lori Perry Nicks provided backup vocals for her. They were a delightfully upbeat presence on the tour, which ran from July 14 to September 18, 1994, and included appearances on The Tonight Show with Jay Leno and a performance at Jess Nicks' venue, Compton Terrace in Phoenix. The reviews are mixed, and the Rorschach test of the reviewers' attitudes toward female artists is clearly visible. "The public's desire to have Nicks conform to the gender trends that flourished in the 1980s and 1990s was unappeased with the 1994 release of Street Angel," a brief examination of her career concluded. "Audiences were bored with Stevie's subtle power demonstrated through songs like 'Rhiannon' and 'Dreams'; they didn't want to look for hidden strength; they wanted overt brashness and a masculine driving energy." "If that's the case [he mentions her oft-stated plan to work into her eighth decade], Street Angel is the beginning of the rest of Nicks' career," said Graff, who is Gary Graff. It does sound like a fresh start. It's straightforward and rocking, with songs about Greta Garbo and Jane Goodall, as well as a guest appearance by Bob Dylan on Nicks' remake of his 'Just Like a Woman'. It's reminiscent of her first solo album, 1981's Bella Donna. And it's hard not to detect a liberating spirit among the 11 songs on Street Angel. The Hartford Courant's music critic called it a "hip return," while the New Jersey Record praised her for rejecting the "cheesy synthesisers" and the Pittsburgh Post-Gazette praised her "smoky-bar-at-3-a.m. voice." It reveals itself to be a formidable weapon once more, glorious in its inability to hit all of the notes and captivating in the emotion it conveys." In five words, Nicks described her experience: "It's not my favourite record." Stephen Davis overexplained the following line: "She said she wanted to go back to the hospital because she hated her new record so much." "It was the saddest, lowest-energy music she'd ever made," she told me. Of course, sad music can be great.

Street Angel marked Nicks' final album for Modern Records. The label filed for bankruptcy in 1999, five years after its initial release. Her next album was released on the Reprise label and distributed by Warner in the United States. The time in between was largely her own; she looked after herself, dieting and exercising and maintaining a strict vocal callisthenics routine, and spending time with friends and family amid occasional creative projects and performances, including, but not limited to, the indispensable Enchanted compilation; an appearance at Woodstock on August 14, 1998 (flying over the crowd in a helicopter thrilled her); several Stevie Nicks & Friends benefit concerts for the Arizona C. She influenced younger balladeers and rockers like Tori Amos and Courtney Love, as well as Isaac Mizrahi and Anna Sui's gothic fashions and gewgaws ("black gossamer and velvet, gargantuan boots and glittering beads").

With her health restored, Nicks was able to pursue her passions, such as writing movie music. She wrote "Twisted" for the summer blockbuster Twister in 1996, accepting the commission after her friend and former assistant Rebecca Alvarez reviewed and approved the script. Both expected the film to set box office records. Nicks stated in the liner notes of Enchanted that the demo was recorded on "March 10, 1996, on a 4-track Tascam by my [new] assistant extraordinaire, Karen Johnston." She gives a few details about her life. "I was living in a beach house overlooking Sunset Boulevard and the Pacific Coast Highway, and beyond that, always . . . the ocean."

Mark Mancina's background score for Twister combines Aaron Copland-inspired "wide open spaces" motifs with generic action-adventure ostinato patterns. Nicks' song began as a demo, with a beatbox and a mandolin overdub, before she called Buckingham. Perhaps he wanted to have fun as well. He turned the song into a powerful closing-credits duet with his own lyrics. Mick Fleetwood also agreed to drum for fun, bringing together three-fifths of Fleetwood Mac for this one-time event. Prior to Buckingham's transposition, the song is playfully macabre, with demons both within and without, "crazy men, crazy women" in need of love. The mandolin "fills the air with colours." It wraps around the voice, leaving the timbre gleaming. The lyrics are incantational, progressing from obsession to possession. The sung line contains no A to B to C transitions. Nicks mentions the film only briefly: "You live for the danger... you play with God." "You" would be the male hero, a storm chaser from the Midwest, but the voice belongs to his wife, Helen Hunt, a university professor and serious scientist. The cat-5 funnel clouds emphasise the forces that pull and push them apart.

The musical close-up, where the dynamic level of the voice is increased, is the best moment in the demo. The drum machine continues to play while Nicks sings about "chasing down the demons." The song could be an exorcism, but it could also be an embrace, because tornadoes use centrifugal force to draw objects into a vortex (while still throwing them out far and wide). The demons come from the Nether, which Nicks mimics with circular phrases.

She recalled the song while working on her most recent solo album, 24 Karat Gold, saying that "when songs go into movies, you might as well dump them out the window as you're driving by because they never get heard." She, Buckingham, and Fleetwood collaborated well, and Fleetwood later organised another Fleetwood Mac reunion to commemorate the twentieth anniversary of Rumours. The band recorded a live show for MTV in Burbank before embarking on a twenty-six-city tour known as The Dance. Davis claims Nicks was "overjoyed with relief" about the reunion because it meant the postponement of her next solo album. It meant she wouldn't have to write a ton of new songs right away. It meant she could enjoy the first-class luxuries of a major Mac tour without having to make any decisions or shoulder the heavy responsibilities of a band leader." This claim is without foundation. It appears to be completely fabricated. Nicks had long regarded Fleetwood Mac as less creative than Petty's band, the Heartbreakers. Producers came and went, so Nicks took on some of the production work herself, renting various studios and recording between tours or individual shows. Making "lots of new songs right away" was not an issue. She experienced a brief bout of writer's block, lasting only a few weeks rather than months. Petty shook it out of her during dinner in Phoenix, asking, "What the hell is wrong with you?" "You can be miserable or you can just get over it." Then he smiled impishly, told her she sounded fantastic, and reminded her of her exceptional songwriting abilities.

Trouble in ShangriLa, her sixth studio album, demonstrated those abilities. Between 1995 and 2001, it was formed on the spur of the moment, with the assistance of old and new friends. Apart from writer's block, she saw no reason to rush through it until her management team became impatient. It went gold only six weeks after its long-awaited release, indicating both her return to form and a successful reboot of her career for the new century. The album was originally titled Trouble in Paradise, after her family's suburban Phoenix neighbourhood, Paradise Valley, and a 1932 film titled Trouble in Paradise (about thieves in disguise, grand hotels, and a diamond purse, with a disapproving communist making a single hilarious appearance), but Randy Newman had already used that name for his 1983 album. Nicks changed "Paradise" to "Shangri-La," a nod to James Hilton's 1933 novel Lost Horizon. Shangri-La is a fictional name for a spiritual enclave east of the Himalayas where residents live a secluded, peaceful, and seemingly endless existence. According to Nicks, the album has a theme—fame isn't all it's cracked up to be, so "be careful what you wish for"—but, aside from the title track, few songs address this.

The majority of the album was produced by John Shanks, but seven other people, including Nicks herself, contributed to it before he was hired. Rick Nowels and Sheryl Crow, who met Nicks at the Grammys in 1996, helped out. Two years later, in Hawaii, she made contact with Nicks. Crow wrote "It's Only Love," one of the songs on Trouble, and helped write others. Nicks hired her as producer in chief until Crow was forced to leave the project due to other obligations. Natalie Maines, lead singer of the Chicks (formerly known as the Dixie Chicks), was suggested as her replacement. "She and I have very similar country voices," said Nicks, "and I could definitely sing with her."

"Too Far from Texas," a song on Trouble in Shangri-La co-written by Nicks and Maines, imagines "love could fly over the ocean" to pursue a man on his way to London while the protagonist pines for him in Houston. Maines' duet with Nicks is simple, heartfelt, and catchy. As a country song, "Too Far from Texas" would complement the Chicks' number-one hit "You Were Mine," which was written by Martie Maguire and Emily Robison, the Chicks' two-third sisters. Although Crow's bass work is frequently highlighted, the truly country twanging guitar work (along with the soulful Hammond organ) imbues the song with greater force. Maines' voice is not as powerful as Nicks', but it sharpens the timbre to give the lyrics more bite; her higher pitch also elevates the song—literally and emotionally. The structure, which includes an emotional payoff and a quick close, is similar to the Chicks' quick endings in songs like "Wide Open Spaces." Maines would later cover "Landslide" (mixed by Crow) on the Chicks' Home (2002), signalling a departure from the pop-country blend that propelled the group to success in favour of an acoustic, bluegrass idiom that better suited Maines' high, lonesome sound. "She's very supportive of other females in the industry," Maines said about Nicks. "I think lots of women are competitive and she really wants you to succeed."

The guitar part in "Bombay Sapphires" is based on Sting's 1993 song "Shape of My Heart." The reference is obvious in the demo but hidden in the final track. Macy Gray, an R&B singer, plays the lead, but Nicks had Sting in mind, telling Q magazine that "the only reason Macy is on the record is because we're managed by the same people." I was going to ask Sting to sing that little high part on Bombay Sapphire[s], but I backed out and asked Macy to do it instead." Gray has a limited vocal range, but she sings with a wide range of emotions, from a childlike whisper to exhausted discontent. She was nearing the pinnacle of her career in 2001, and management must have considered her marketability when recommending her to Nicks. The song "Bombay Sapphires" was recorded in three takes: the first was too R&B, the second was too "dirge-like," and the third was "its funky little reggae self." The subject is not gin (dubbed "the mother's ruin"), but Nicks expected Bombay Sapphire fans to make the connection. The use of plurals in the title prevented copyright infringement. She wrote the song in Maui, and the lyrics describe how rejuvenated she felt in that aqua-blue environment after The Dance tour. It's a cool response to Fleetwood Mac's scandalous fecundity—bright and beautiful, with no trace of shadow. Sarah McLachlan, who had previously moved from the alternative singer-songwriter scene to the musical mainstream, was also involved. She was irritated by the industry's sexism, particularly the refusal to program and schedule more than one female artist at a time. In response, she founded Lilith Fair in the late 1990s, which was named after the divine entity of kabbalist mysticism. It was a multistage travelling production similar to Lollapalooza, but "women-centric" (rather than "women-exclusive," as men were barred from participating in the bands). Before and after Lilith Fair's three-year run, there was expected backlash from the male rock establishment and Christian right-wing media. Misogynists targeted Trouble in Shangri-La for its "Lilith Fairian posse of special guests," highlighting both the festival's significance and Nicks' "protective attitude" toward Crow and other young female artists. "It had taken a long time for [Nicks's] own status to be restored," popular music expert Lucy O'Brien writes, and she helped keep her protégées from losing theirs.

The Nicks-McLachlan collaboration was unexpected, but it became the album's centrepiece. Pierre Marchand, McLachlan's producer, who Nicks hired for the song "Love Is," was delayed crossing the border into the United States from Canada. When he couldn't record with Nicks in Los Angeles, he suggested she visit Vancouver, where he introduced her to McLachlan. He was aware that she admired Sarah McLachlan's 1994 song "Possession," which had a turbulent history. The lyrics were inspired by poems sent to McLachlan by a devoted fan, as well as her own traumatic interactions with him. The stalker sued her for stealing his words after the song was released, but she committed suicide before the case could be tried. The song is eerie, unearthly, and strangely soothing, with a presence and ambiance that recalls the popular witchcraft films The Craft and Practical Magic from the 1990s. McLachlan and Nicks appear to be tuned into the distinctly feminine energy of the era. Crow and Nicks' duet, "If You Ever Did Believe," appeared on the Practical Magic soundtrack.

McLachlan sings background vocals and plays piano on Marchand's wonderful song "Love Is". Nicks' ennui-laden recitation of the words is accompanied by breathing sounds, staccato "oohs" above the bass line in the third and fifth measures, and a polished interwoven harmonic texture. The song Nicks and Buckingham argued about, the fourth track on Say You Will, found new life as the theme for a 2003 Friends episode titled "The One with the Soap Opera Party." The title perfectly fits the context of the song, but it does not excuse Buckingham's condescending refusal to recognize a change in tense as perfectly appropriate for internal dialogue. The tenth track, "Smile at You," is from the Tusk sessions. Nicks originally recorded it with friends Annie McLoone and Tom Moncrieff, according to Ken Caillat. She "couldn't get [the song] past Lindsey," Caillat writes, due to Moncrieff's "smoking guitar solo." To his credit, Caillat saw it as a "potential classic," in which Nicks' simmering resentment erupts into rage as a "vicious answer song to Lindsey." He never worked on it for Tusk or, as was briefly considered, Mirage. The song evolved over time, reflecting the Nicks-Buckingham creative dialogue. When Fleetwood Mac recorded Say You Will, Buckingham had already left Nicks' life. The five leaked takes of "Smile" by Tusk, two by Mirage, and the final version by Say You Will range from hostile to defiant to circumspect. Some of the demos resemble "Sisters of the Moon," while the final take incorporates prickly acoustic guitar and shamanistic percussion. The throbbing bass line returns to "The Chain" by John McVie. In the Fleetwood Mac universe, unresolved feelings are preferable to resolved feelings, and when Nicks sings "I shouldn't be here," it's hard not to believe she's over the lack of closure.

"Illume" tells the story of the September 11, 2001 terrorist attacks on the World Trade Center and the Pentagon. On that day, Nicks was in Toronto as part of the Shangri-La tour. The air traffic shutdown and blackout that followed the destruction of the Twin Towers forced her to cancel shows in Rochester (September 12) and New York City (September 14). She wanted to cancel all of the dates for this month and the following month. Petty and Henley persuaded her that performing would benefit a beleaguered public. She returned to California a month later and wrote the poem that became the song "Illume."

It's simply a matter of making it. I was sitting there, thinking about the horrible tragedies of October 2001, and there was only me and the candle in the room. I have a thing for candles. And my heart was still heavy from everything, and I had no idea what was going to happen, so we were all confused.

I didn't set out to write a song about 9/11; it just happened. It begins, "Illume, says the candle that I burn, a reflection in the window," and that is the song's inspiration. And let me tell you, my heart was heavy and full at the time, and I was perplexed. And there are a few other things...

The Say You Will tour was a squabble, and Nicks quickly abandoned it in favour of a more pleasant concert series with Henley, the successful Gold Dust solo tour, and another tour to commemorate the release of the management-driven compilation album Crystal Visions. Nicks became more involved with charitable causes. Her father has passed away. She remained with her mother for a few more years. In 2006, she attended the Arcadia High School Class of 1966's 40th reunion at the Westin Pasadena. Despite having spent her senior year of high school at Menlo-Atherton, she accepted the invitation to reminisce. She met Robin Snyder in Arcadia, where she performed in Changing Times. "You know what?" asked someone she used to know. You have not changed in the least. Stevie, you're still our little girl. "Because it was the nicest thing anyone had said to me, that I'm still the same," tears welled up. Because I've always tried very hard to remain the person I was before joining Fleetwood Mac and not become a very arrogant and obnoxious, conceited, bitchy chick, as many do, and I believe I've been very successful." She read all of the Twilight novels as soon as they came out. Romantic stories about star-crossed lovers, vampires, eternal life, impossible love, and the pleasures and dangers of corrupted innocence. Much had changed, of course, but her fascination with teenagers getting into mischief because of their "desire, will, and imagination" persisted.

In 2011, Nicks released In Your Dreams, her seventh album and first in a decade, with Dave Stewart writing roughly half of the songs. Glen Ballard, whose credits include rock, pop, films (Batman, The Polar Express), and musicals (Ghost, Back to the Future), co-produced it. Stewart and Ballard hired a large number of session musicians to replace the demos' programmed loop parts. Simon Smith was part of this group. He spent two hours playing bass on "Everybody Loves You" at Ballard's studio and recalls that the lyrics changed between the demo and the final version. He has never met Nicks.

On the cover of In Your Dreams, Nicks stands behind a translucent orb next to a white horse in a glade—an unapologetically innocent romantic imagining. Less innocent is her summer reading-inspired song, "Moonlight (a Vampire's Dream)." Jonathan Keafe took issue with it, stating, "Inspired by her viewing [sic] of The Twilight Saga: New Moon while on tour[,] it boasts exactly the same degree of depth as Stephenie Meyer's vapid, wooden prose." "Even worse is 'New Orleans,' with a howlingly bad chorus that finds Nicks singing, 'I want to dress up / I want to wear beads / I want to wear feathers and lace / I want to brush by Anne Rice,' with an inexplicable reverence," he says about the song's fifth verse. Because the melody lifts at the end of each line, the last word in those lines is overemphasised, giving the song an obnoxious, stilted cadence. It's possibly the worst song in Nicks' entire discography, reducing New Orleans culture to Bourbon Street and vampire mythology."

"New Orleans" isn't meant to be taken seriously, and "Moonlight" shouldn't be dismissed so lightly, especially given its connection to the four Twilight novels and films. Bella, the hero, is a seventeen-year-old from Arizona, and in New Moon, the second book in the tetralogy, she meets, or believes she meets, her grandmother, unless she is seeing herself as her grandmother's age. Nicks' song starts with the line, "Some call her strange lady from the mountains." She is referring to her own cousin, Alice from "Alice." Jenny Turner, an expert on Meyer's novels, notes the obvious parallel with Dorian Gray. Then there's the central dilemma of Bella's relationship with Edward. He maintains his distance from her and encourages her to keep her clothes on because neither of them will look as cute from the other side. The bottom line is that he is a beautiful monster until they have sex, after which he transforms into something else. Nicks does not dwell on this specific negative. Her song shines, and the video is a simple affair, featuring her backup singers, slender man Waddy Wachtel, Stewart dressed as a magician, an owl, and a few session musicians.

I suppose the electronic distortion represents dysrhythmia, but if "Moonlight" is vampiric, then so is the entire popular music industry. Everything in the carefully crafted song has its proper place. It is the pinnacle. Bella recognizes Edward, an undead orphan with flawless skin. He is a studio technician who has avoided the limelight. Meyer portrays him as both artificial and ideal, making him appealing to a girl who despises fake people and things. Edward, like fashion magazines, cannot be avoided. Fake things are ideal images are dead things, so our world, like Meyer's, is full of vampires.

The Gothic was said to focus readers' deepest fears about the future: blood-sucking aristocrats; mills, engines, new technology, with its way of blurring the line between the human and the non-human; infant mortality, post-mortem flatus, afterlife doubts, and, of course, the problem of death. We no longer need to go to the movies to see life transformed into images of immortal perfection; they flicker all around us, stripped of the animal and filled with plastics. As a result, the question isn't so much about going into the "labyrinthine realm of undeath" as it is about whether anyone can ever truly leave it. Hello, and welcome to the Hotel California. You and Bella both believe you have returned the keys and are ready to leave, but you are still a guest.

Is Nicks willing to go, despite her self-consciousness and image-consciousness? She sings as if no time has passed in her career, and she has no remorse for her enduring love of things that others dismiss as adolescent. Womanhood is frequently defined as being ashamed of girlish things, but could maturity also honour the younger self's feelings and loves? The girl does not have to die so that the woman can live.

Nicks reconnected with Stewart five years before the release of In Your Dreams, when he asked her to do an interview for the pilot episode of the HBO series Off the Record, which he hosts. Nicks gave a fifteen-minute rendition of "Rhiannon" for the broadcast. Stewart then wrote her a song: "Everyone loves you, but you're alone," the chorus begins. She took to it, added the missing verse material, and invited him over to record it in her private studio, utilising the acoustics in her Pacific Palisades home's rotunda and winding staircase. Stewart searched through a book of poems she had accumulated over the years for additional songs. "I don't know a thousand chords, and Dave doesn't have a book of forty poems," she said of their thirteen-track album, which they worked on intermittently between February and December 2010. "When you put those two things together, you have this amazing amount of wisdom and knowledge." Stewart had a long-standing interest in film—as a child, he traded a gold bracelet he found on the street for an eight-millimetre camera—and proposed making a film out of their collaboration.86 The story of each song's creation was enhanced by footage from the HBO episode and old photographs (of the Pasadena tavern her father owned and her grandfather frequented).

It had been a lovely months-long reunion, complete with dress-up parties, masquerade masks, running kids, barking Yorkies, and Reese Witherspoon sipping a cocktail. (The title "Cheaper Than Free" is derived from Witherspoon's casual invitation to Stewart to stay at her Nashville home.) "Suddenly everybody started turning into characters," Stewart wrote in his biography, "influenced, no doubt, by the house and Stevie's obsession with Edgar Allan Poe [the song 'Annabel Lee' appears on In Your Dreams]." People dressed in Edwardian attire began to appear. My daughters, Kaya and Indya, were dressed as spooky little characters, holding owls and walking through the halls.

When it was time for work, the headdresses, boas, and flowing trains were put away. The documentary confirms Nicks' extraordinary ear and poor eyesight, as she changes glasses and reads lyrics with a magnifier. Karen Johnston, her assistant, kept the grand pianos in tune and helped prepare the studio for the growing number of guest musicians. Nicks called Buckingham for help with one of the tracks, then argued with him about her musicianship. Fleetwood also appeared, as did Mike Campbell, Waddy Wachtel, and Neale Heywood. Nicks' backup singers include two violinists, four Hammond organists, several bassists and percussionists, and a single mandolinist.

Rumours' single, "Secret Love," is a demo that did not make the final cut. The protagonist seeks solace from a former lover who believes there is still hope for reconciliation. Nick's relaxed, calm-in-the-middle-of-the-storm The singing contrasts with the sharply focused, jangling accompaniment. She spent more time on "Soldier's Angel." In 2005, I was inspired by a visit to wounded Iraq War veterans in Washington, DC, as well as news of a massacre of British soldiers in the same conflict. Nicks rehearses the song in the documentary on her red satin couch by the fireplace and in the rotunda, in an environment of extreme privilege—the privilege of being completely shielded from the world's sorrows. Nicks is dangerously close to calling herself out on it. The song's narrator is the soldier's "girl" as well as his "memory," "mother," and "widow." She protests war because the soldier's sacrifice has earned her the right to do so. The music is dirge-like, with the guitar's falling fifth transitioning into a falling sixth as it nears the end of a descending tetrachord—a musical symbol of lament. During the verses, the bass drum trudges. In the chorus, the texture lightens, bringing "ghostly shadows... back into the light." Buckingham, who co-wrote the song, harmonised in thirds with Nicks in the chorus, evoking the starkest moments from their debut album from 1973.

Wide Sargasso Sea, published in 1966, depicts abject suffering set against a backdrop of oppressive heat. The protagonist, Antoinette Conway, is the Creole child of the owner of a former sugar plantation in Coulibri, Jamaica. Her childhood home has fallen into disrepair since slavery was abolished. Abuse devastates her sense of self. "I knew the time of day when, even though it is hot and blue and there are no clouds, the sky can have a very black look," Antoinette says in one of the novel's most famous lines. (In contrast, Nick describes the ocean as "so heavy, so big, so massive, and so dangerous. It simply makes me happy. "It is far superior to Prozac." Antoinette marries an Englishman who brags about his infidelity, changes her name, and confines her to an attic at his remote English mansion, Thornton Hall. Grace Poole, a character from Charlotte Brontë's 1847 novel Jane Eyre, becomes Antoinette's malevolent guardian. Wide Sargasso Sea is a feminist, anti-colonialist prequel that interweaves two transatlantic stories.

Nicks' lyrics allude to Antoinette's distrust of her husband, as well as the novel's final chapter, in which Antoinette escapes her cell by burning down her captor's house, just as emancipated slaves had done to her childhood home. Stewart is responsible for the superslick production that undermines effect, emotion, and sentiment; slapping one screeching guitar solo on top of another; the synthesiser interjections and abrupt shift from hushed romantic ballad to din-filled blues rock; the heartbeat rhythm of the coda; encouraging Nicks to sing with a Nashville twang; and demonstrating that he had no idea what to do with the text. Sheen was probably an appropriate choice for the song about Stephenie Meyer. It's not appropriate for this one.

Nicks was fascinated by the voodoo scenes in the novel and film, as well as the alleged drumming of cannibals. "When those drums stop," she continues, "you'd better start running." That's an unusual thing to say about such a gentle track. The gothic legend takes a backseat on the album, with the exception of the track she rescued from her youth, "Annabel Lee." Rhys' melancholy streak—"the sense of loss, and a consequent sense of being at a loss"—did not rub off on Nicks, despite the fact that Robin had left her life and both of her parents had passed away by 2012. Tom Petty would also leave, signalling the end of the rock-star lifestyle, with the exception of the part about living in the moment all the time.

On July 21, 2017, Lana Del Rey and Nicks released a stunning duet titled "Beautiful People, Beautiful Problems". Petty died ten weeks later, on October 2, 2017, from an accidental overdose of painkillers for a bone fracture. He slipped and cracked his hip during a tour rehearsal with the Heartbreakers, after deciding to postpone hip replacement surgery. "Honestly, my audience is what keeps me going," he said, fatefully. Standing onstage night after night with a guitar slung over his right shoulder made the fracture worse, and it eventually broke. According to a report in the Los Angeles Times, "Petty struggled with depression, anxiety, and insomnia, as well as pain from the hip fracture, as evidenced by substances the coroner found in his system when he died: fentanyl and oxycodone (painkillers); alprazolam (Xanax) and temazepam (to treat anxiety and insomnia); and citalopram, an antidepressant." The litany evokes images of a tortured male genius, mythologizing Petty.

Fans and family members were once again left wondering what could have gone differently. Dana York, his second wife and now widow, stated that "he was very stubborn" and "would still be with us" if he had undergone hip surgery rather than driving. Nicks performed a solo show with him, which was released after his death, and stated, "Even now, when I talk about him onstage, I talk about him like he's not dead—because I don't want him to be dead." So I talk to him as if he's still down the street [she used to live next to him in Encino] and I can call him. I'm glad this show was recorded before he died because I believe it would have influenced how I spoke about everything if he had died first. There would have been a sad pang. And it was all very enjoyable.

She enjoyed his company and his music, which spoke to her in a straightforward and enjoyable manner. "It's really easy for Tom and me to be theatrical on stage," she once told MTV, drawing comparisons to "Fred Astaire and Ginger Rogers."

Perhaps she was thinking about "Let's Face the Music and Dance," Ginger's fabulous feathered gown, or the paradoxical authenticity of her and Fred's duets, the genuine moments among the scripted ones. Perhaps she was recalling a famous line from Texas state treasurer (and later governor) Ann Richards' keynote speech at the 1988 Democratic National Convention. She advocated for women's political participation, saying, "If you give us a chance, we can perform." Ginger Rogers, after all, accomplished everything Fred Astaire did. She just did it in high heels, backwards."

Nicks still feels Petty's presence in her life, as she recently told Tavi Gevinson in a New Yorker interview about their connection, even on the night he died:

I understand Tom. I was up late watching TV in my apartment, which has a view that goes all the way to the pier and back to Point Dume. And then I looked over to the right and saw this little red dot heading down toward Malibu, so I went over to the window and just stood there, watching it come all the way up and then slow down before coming to a halt on the street ahead of me. And after Tom died, I realised he was in that ambulance. Nicks participated in Fleetwood Mac reunions while pursuing her solo career until the band performed at the MusiCares Person of the Year ceremony at Radio City Music Hall in January 2018. Lorde, Haim, Harry Styles, Alison Krauss, OneRepublic, and other artists paid tribute to Fleetwood Mac, making the evening feel upbeat for the audience. The band took their places on stage, with Fleetwood taking the lead; Nicks, as usual, came in last, following Buckingham. With the exception of the reticent John McVie, they all spoke, praising MusiCares for raising $7 million that night to assist struggling musicians. Buckingham, the Prospero of the Fleetwood Mac storm, reflected on the band's complex history and the love that underpins it all. During Nicks' self-effacing turn at the podium, Fleetwood and Christine McVie pretended to waltz before acknowledging the passing of the luminaries, most notably Petty, who had lit and kept her path shining. The curtain was drawn in anticipation of the band's mini-set, which Nicks promised would pique everyone's interest. Backstage, the tension was palpable. Buckingham mocked the choice of "Rhiannon" as walk-on music. He made it clear that he despised the old material; he had returned from self-imposed exile with new material, which the group refused to play.

After the show, Nicks' manager, Irving Azoff, informed Buckingham that Nicks would never perform onstage with him again. Nothing was fun anymore; the debates were old, never-ending, and, worst of all, boring. They had both spoken a lot. He said it, she said it, and he said it too. It was over. Buckingham felt underappreciated. And, yes, he had mostly ignored Bella Donna and Nicks' other solo albums, including those to which he contributed. He was unimpressed with her creativity, voice, and how it related to the experiences of people—particularly women—who did not run record labels or decide what would be heard on the radio or streamed. If he had given "Joan of Arc" a chance as an arranger, performer, and producer whose instincts Nicks respected, it could have topped the charts. That did not happen, and neither did the Buckingham Nicks sequel, no matter how fantastic it would have been.

Buckingham, like his brother Greg and father Morris, died from a heart attack in February 2019. Kristen Messner, a photographer and interior designer who married him in 2000, provided regular updates on his recovery from emergency triple bypass surgery, and Nicks wrote Buckingham a note urging him to take care of himself. The ventilator that saved his life harmed his vocal cords, slightly lowering his voice; his straight-up, socket-finger hair turned grey. He announced a club tour for June 2021 and released a self-titled album featuring the calming single "I Don't Mind." Consolation, on the other hand, does not sell music as well as dysfunction, and Buckingham attempted to bait Nicks in the Los Angeles Times, New York Times, and Rolling Stone—and all of the publications that aggregated them—by labelling her "lonely" and "low energy." The pigtail-pulling hasn't gotten her too enthusiastic. Meanwhile, Messner confirmed that she had filed for divorce. That, too, has been portrayed as acrimonious.

No one questions Buckingham's abilities, and a slew of blog posts and YouTube comments argue that if Nicks had stayed with him, her music would have done better commercially, despite her induction into the Rock & Roll Hall of Fame in 2019 and subsequent $100 million sale of the rights to her catalogue, name, and likeness to the publishing and talent management firm Primary Wave. Buckingham recently sold his entire catalogue, which includes the platinum-selling music he wrote for Fleetwood Mac as well as his solo efforts, which range from delicate acoustic tracks to garage rock, generic pop, and covers of his father's 45s. Some of the songs are filled with complaints, while others are coldly indifferent. He expressed his displeasure with Mick Fleetwood's gossipy memoirs in the 1992 song "Wrong." Fleetwood is known as "Young Mr. Rockcock." Boys will be boys.

CHAPTER 7
24 KARAT GOLD

Girls can also be divas.

Stevie Nicks has been compared to legendary women on stage and screen such as Judy Garland, Billie Holiday, Dolly Parton, and Barbra Streisand. She chose to align herself with two other celebrated divas instead: Greta Garbo and Mabel Normand. The latter is less well-known, but Nicks believes it deserves more attention. Nicks' eighth and most recent album, which represents the pinnacle of her comeback, features a stream-of-consciousness song about Normand.

It's called 24 Karat Gold and subtitled Songs from the Vault, and it contains demos and drafts of songs she'd almost forgotten about until stolen copies began to surface online, some from a suitcase of cassettes her ex-husband Kim Anderson had sold at a yard sale. Nicks, who avoids the Internet (she writes with pen and paper and only uses her iPhone as a phone), found out too late that her archive had been stolen; bootleggers had assembled their own versions of 24 Karat Gold. Her lawyers determined that she needed to reclaim her copyright, so the archive was converted into a vault and 24 Karat Gold, a collection of new songs layered on top of old and new. Dave Stewart and Waddy Wachtel co-produced the album with her at Nashville's Blackbird Studios, influenced by Sound City, producer Keith Olsen, and Buckingham Nicks' electroacoustic sound. It's a polished rawness album, a bold, rich mix of pre- and post-coffee-plant tapes that investigates how things could have been different. In this sense, it is a revelation rather than a reinvention, which is unacceptable to a true diva.

The album received mixed reviews, but that didn't matter because it was intended for Nicks' longtime fans. She began her tour on October 25, 2016 at Talking Stick Resort Arena. She confesses that she's "a little freaked out [from nerves]—just a little—but I'm in my hometown, Phoenix, where I wrote a lot of my songs." She began by opening for The Pretenders and went on to become commercial music's mercurial genetrix—upmarket urban siren, downmarket desert heart—for listeners ranging from "15 to 93." Joe Thomas recorded Stevie Nicks' 24 Karat Gold the Concert over two nights in Indianapolis and Pittsburgh. It's almost as interested in Nicks' biographical stories (including generous tributes to Prince and Keith Olsen) as it is in her music, though Thomas edited out some of her diva-ish "stream of consciousness" longueurs. The film was supposed to be released on October 21, 2020, in 900 theatres worldwide, but the pandemic ruined the festivities. Instead, it ended up online. The Daily Californian described it as "wonderful" but "too long." The Digital Journal referred to it as "unforgettable."

24 Karat Gold consists of fourteen tracks, thirteen of which are remakes of songs written between 1969 and 1995. The bleak demo from the Rock a Little sessions, "Night Gallery," was left out; its time has not yet come. The deluxe edition includes two additional tracks: "Twisted" and "Watch Chain." The latter's demo, from the 1970s, features Nicks doubling on vocals over a reggae-inspired guitar lick and a laid-back beat. Mick Fleetwood offered the analogy. He liked watch chains, even when he was dressed in faded blue jeans, as the lyrics indicate. The origins of the clumsier alternate title, "Watch Devil," are unknown, but there is plenty of folklore about clocks and the ringing of the hours being the devil's work. It's a seventies song that sounds like a sixties song, with lyrics about old age presented as remembered now in an ironic way.

Bella Donna released "Blue Water" in the early 1980s. Nicks recorded it with the Nashville trio Lady A (formerly Lady Antebellum), with whom she had been exchanging songs for five years and had even performed at the Academy of Country Music Awards together. Lady A's harmonies significantly brighten the texture, bringing Christian "soul" to Nicks' upbeat Hawaiian Pacific ode. Dave Haywood's guitar curlicues suggest different, less austere melodic accompaniment options. The piano-vocal version Nicks recorded for her first Rolling Stone cover story since 1981 is intimate, but the Lady A transposition enhances the romantic nature imagery by pushing past the text's narcissism (the water stares back at her while she waits for her gypsy). The harmonisation is like the ethereal opening and closing of a blue water lily.

"Blue Water" describes a situation in flux, perhaps indefinitely, and Nicks transforms instability into sound. It's an issue for critics like

Jim Farber, who sees the looseness of 24 Karat gold as a flaw: "Unlike her beautifully pruned Fleetwood Mac work, many songs on her latest solo album fray at the seams or wander outside the confines of an ideal melody."" There are a few must-have tracks on the album, but key parts have lyrics that wobble awkwardly on their beats. Those flaws and indulgences, however, shed more light on Nicks' character and concerns than ever before." Farber does not elaborate on these concerns, but the tides and whirlpools mentioned in "Blue Water" show different views of time. There is both a pull into and a denial of the abyss, as Michel de Montaigne put it: "Our desires incessantly grow young again; we are always re-beginning to live." Recent interviews with Nicks have emphasised the "adventure just around the corner" (a phrase Stewart used) and the fact that she has never had a clear artistic goal to strive for. Uncertainty and discursiveness frustrate music executives, but they are the stuff of art. In general, commercial entertainment appreciates the fantastical messiness of dreams as long as it is cleaned up before the end. Nicks had stopped cleaning a long time ago.

Nicks' voice has changed, but this is beneficial to the remake of the 1971 song "Lady." The 2014 version takes advantage of her current voice's richer lower-range timbre. She has essentially abandoned her mezzo-soprano register from the 1980s and 1970s, when she could sing an octave and a half above and below middle C with her trademark fierceness and tenderness intact. Her sound has gradually become compressed as a result of road wear and tear and the passage of time: She didn't have years of professional training, so she figured out the tricks of the trade with the help of her friend Robin Snyder: slowing and pausing rhythms, shrouding the thinnest thread of a phrase in breath, increasing and decreasing pressure on discrete pitches—depending on the points she wanted to make.

In the official video for "Lady," she portrays herself as a performer from another era rather than a new type of singer. She sings without a band in a theatre with a royal red curtain, plainly and directly at the mic and in the rhythm of a cradle song, a digital age superstar attempting to break into a Nashville old-time music venue. "Lady" is modest and reserved. It's not immediately catchy; it takes a few listens to notice the gradual increase in emotional investment from the first verse and pre-chorus to the soaring breakout moment at the heart of the song—"what is to become of me?" Nicks's older self understands the answer to her younger self's question. She steps back for the second verse, which is a modified version of the first. She takes a tired pause after singing "knockin' on doors when there's nobody there." She then gives one final push before the lights turn off.

One of the songs features music written by Dire Straits' Mark Knopfler. Cal, a brooding 1984 film set in Belfast during Northern Ireland's religious war, served as its inspiration. The plot revolves around the doomed, Tristan and Isolde-style romance between the Catholic Cal, an IRA lansquenet, and the widow of a Protestant police officer murdered by the IRA, in which Cal plays a role. Cal tries to conceal himself from both those seeking his arrest and his own conscience. It is impossible, just as Marcella, his widow, cannot suppress her feelings of love and hatred for him. Liam O'Flynn on uilleann pipes contributes significantly to Knopfler's Celtic-influenced soundtrack. It's typically beautiful, haunting, and reserved, reflecting both the film's setting and the characters' psychological states. Nicks' arrangement replaces the pipes with six-string and twelve-string guitars panned to opposite sides. The final track on 24 Karat Gold appears to be dedicated to one of the men in her life, but it also fits the film because it describes a love that "no one understands" and includes a reference to the Irish sea. The song, "She Loves Him Still," is a simple ballad with a spoken-word bridge to the chorus. There is also a cover of a song by Vanessa Lee Carlton, whose career was influenced by Nicks' spiritual and creative direction. Carlton rose to prominence in 2002 when she released the single "A Thousand Miles" from her album Be Not Nobody. It has now become her trademark. Carlton has continued to perform and record albums, totaling six, and has opened for Nicks, whom she regards as a friend and protégée. Barbara Nicks, Nicks' mother, enjoyed Carlton's 2011 song "Carousel," which inspired Nicks to cover it with Carlton as singer and instrumentalist. (Nicholas' niece, Jessica, also performs on the track.) The original version is the opening track on Carlton's 2011 album Rabbits on the Run. It was recorded in the acoustically perfect "wood room" of Peter Gabriel's Real World Studios near Bath. The video has the appearance of a fashion shoot; rural life has never looked more chic. The vamp mimics both the spinning of the carousel and the chord progression of Cyndi Lauper's more solemn "True Colours." Nicks cuts the children's chorus.

Ann Marie Calhoun, a violinist and fiddler, brings nuance to Nicks' version. She gave a traditional performance of Nicks' In Your Dreams. In "Carousel," she honours Barbara Nicks by demonstrating her knowledge of American folk traditions. (Calhoun's father, a self-described hillbilly and Pocahontas descendant, played the banjo; her sister is an accomplished bluegrass musician; and she has performed Appalachian music.)12 The carousel metaphor is used in the text to represent the intricacies of relationships, their presences and absences. The original has an Edenic Enya-like gloss, but Nicks and Calhoun, who obtained it from various sources, prefer corn syrup sweetness. She once rode the rails with an African American ensemble specialising in Afro-Appalachian music in Gordonsville, Virginia. She has also recorded bluegrass, appeared on the soundtracks of films about superheroes (Man of Steel) and inhumans (12 Years a Slave), and collaborated with Damian Marley and Ringo Starr. She embodies cosmopolitan hillbillyness, similar to Barbara's daughter (A.J.'s granddaughter).

The album's title track creates a hypnotic vamp with a tripping, chick-a-boom bass pattern and precise eighth notes in the backbeat. The harmonic progression resembles the 24-karat-gold song "Dreams." The guitar playing is typical of the genre, with a sparkling exchange between a clean single-coil and an overdriven one in the bridge to the final chorus. The song alternates between verse and chorus, but on the 1979 demo (intended for Bella Donna, not Tusk), the contrast between the two sections is broken by a cadential move beneath the chorus's trailing lines, which ask, "What kind of freedom? "What kind of game?"

On the demo, the piano and guitar lines arpeggiate a pair of major chords, and the singing is clipped in a specific range. "You said you might be coming back to town," the strophe-ending declaration, is based on a single pitch, F, that does not appear elsewhere in the song. The threat or promise of returning to town (Nicks' delivery combines hope and fear) is typical of country rock and could have been used in any of her songs. Then there is a shift from major to minor for "let me be... face down" on the ground "in the rain." When she repeats the declaration ("set me free"), the connection between melody and accompaniment is severed, and a F major seventh chord is introduced, with the E pointing outside the harmonic confines until the astonishing moment when the song folds back on itself, elaborating, according to the lyrics, a collapse of the world into the wind. Nicks says, "Here comes the cold chill," and the opening vamp reappears. The vamp's two major chords are brittle and harsh, unlike anything you'd hear in popular music. The produced version's snarling bass conveys that frostiness, but the line "here comes the cold chill" is no longer sung. It belongs entirely to the demo.

Although gold is meant to be saved and hoarded rather than spent, it is used as currency in love songs. The "golden wings in the sunset" suggest both flight and death, and the protagonist asks to be brought "back" from the horizon because there was "no one, out there" (a hollowly harmonised line that sounds lonelier). The phrase "24 karat gold" is punctuated by "chain of chains," which is unsustainable as a reference to Fleetwood Mac's ever-expanding family, Hollywood's dream factory, or a best-selling album—unless all of those references are combined in a golden excess of signification. The chimes, triangle, and reverberating backing singers add a twinkle to the chorus. According to 24 Karat Gold, the most important aspects of Nicks' music are the raw ore: fragmented melodies, half-realised ideas, loosely organised declamations, cut-and-paste structures, and playfulness and whimsy (both expressive and referential). Loretta Lynn, a country singer, and Janis Joplin, a rock musician, both appear. Unlike Nicks' first two solo albums, which emphasised emotional intensity over nuance, the abandoned songs recovered for 24 Karat Gold reveal her imagination through disconnected poetic images and asynchronous melodic accompaniment relationships. Her self-awareness is present throughout the album, most notably on the song dedicated to her newly discovered alter ego, described as a "mess" in Farber's mixed bag of a review.

The implication is that the song, "Mabel Normand," required a more involved producer than Stewart or Wachtel. There are shockingly few female producers in the industry (only 2.6 percent of the Billboard Hot 100 songs charted in 2020 featured women behind the console), and Nicks has yet to collaborate with one. Sheryl Crow's role in Trouble in Shangri-La is an exception. However, it's possible that this song, about the short-lived actress Mabel Normand (1892-1930), is intended to sound like this. Perhaps Nicks intended it to be a total disaster.

Biographers have described Normand as both flawless and deeply flawed. Normand played the clown and pretended to be aristocratic, but she also had an introverted, melancholy personality. Despite having studied Henri Bergson, Sigmund Freud, and Oscar Wilde, the "I don't care girl," the actor of "pure emotion," was unable to avoid the company of crass "slapstick guys." She rose to prominence on the silver screen before sound—and even before scripts. She died (of tuberculosis) just as the silent era was coming to an end, her reputation tarnished by intrigue, self-abuse, and gossip, and she was forever linked to Gloria Swanson's disturbing portrayal in the Hollywood horror film Sunset Boulevard.

Normand was born before most of the boulevard was built, and he came from the far north shore of Staten Island, America. Her father, Claude, worked as a carpenter and pianist at a retirement home for sailors, while her mother, Mille, sang. After boarding school, Normand modelled clothing, endorsed cosmetics, and posed for lantern slides before lying about her age to land an acting job with Vitagraph Studios in New York for $25 per week (equivalent to $680 in today's currency). She relocated to the West Coast and Keystone Studios in Echo Park, Los Angeles, as "a frisky colt who knew no bridle."

Normand produced dozens of eight- and fifteen-minute slapstick comedies in which he jumped off cliffs and was tethered to railroad tracks. Her on-screen collaborators included Charlie Chaplin, whose early career she helped advance but who vastly outearned and eclipsed her as a star, and Roscoe "Fatty" Arbuckle, with whom she appeared in a series of low-key romantic comedies such as Mabel and Fatty's Wash Day (1915). Normand demonstrated more emotional and psychological depth in later feature films, but she was never taken seriously enough. Her specialty was making practical jokes. Mickey (1918) portrayed her as a pulchritudinous tomboy triumphant over adversity, and it was the only film released by the company under her name. Normand, like Mary Pickford, displayed an almost unprecedented level of ambition for a woman at the time, but she was harassed on her way to the top. Mack Sennett, a producer, director, and studio head, proposed to her while cheating on her, and she nearly died when her romantic rival hit her in the head with a vase. In reality, slapstick can be deadly.

Her later years in Los Angeles exposed the negative aspects of the Roaring Twenties film industry. On September 5, 1921, Arbuckle was arrested in connection with the assault and death of 26-year-old actor Virginia Rappe in a San Francisco hotel. Despite his eventual acquittal—there was no assault; Rapper died of alcohol poisoning—the trial ruined Arbuckle's career and harmed Normand's reputation. The press sensationalism the case, as it did with the unsolved murder of film director William Desmond Taylor on February 2, 1922. (The case inspired a forensic subfield known as Taylorology.) Taylor loved her as much as the other men did, but in a more chivalrous manner, even keeping a locket with a picture of the two of them inside. Normand was the last person to see him alive, having allegedly sought his help in overcoming her cocaine addiction, but the extent of her addiction, if she had one, is disputed by her great-nephew, who claims that her biographers were mistaken in believing what the tabloids said about her during the Roaring Twenties. He claims that gin was more of her special helper than cocaine, ignoring the fact that both were illegal during that decade. The Harrison Act of 1914 severely restricted the drug's distribution, but doctors could continue to prescribe it. As journalists warned of the dangers of addiction, the Miller Act of 1922 targeted importers and the Andean cocaine trade: "Self-respect and hope are dead, and a cruel and dominant selfishness has taken their place." He must have the drug or face unimaginable torture. "Life is the drug." Taylor is said to have promised to go after Normand's suppliers, and it is suspected, though not confirmed, that the suppliers took out a life insurance policy on him. Normand was devastated by his death. Another horror struck two years later. On New Year's Day 1924, Normand was invited to Courtland Dines' apartment, a boisterous Denver oil tycoon who was "playing the field in Hollywood." Despite being betrothed to another actress, Edna Purviance, he had developed feelings for Normand and had even taken her out on a few occasions without her knowledge. The evening devolved into chaos, so Normand called her chauffeur, Horace Green, for help. When the chauffeur arrived, Dines refused to let him in, resulting in an argument in which Dines threatened to "brain" him with a whiskey bottle. The chauffeur had brought Normand's Colt pistol with him for protection and fired three times, hitting Dines in the ear and lung. During the trial, it was revealed that he was a chain gang escapee who went by the alias Joe Kelly. Normand refused to defend him, saying, "Shush, the poor boob was nuts," in a high-pitched, dry sarcastic tone. "He was just one of the servants, and he was treated accordingly." I didn't even treat him like one of my many reliable chauffeurs. And by the way, I did not hire this egg. That was handled by my secretary." The chauffeur chastised Normand for her excessive alcohol consumption. Dines did not testify, and the chauffeur was acquitted.

Normand died many years before Nicks was born, but there are striking similarities in some photographs. Some of Normand's film titles could even serve as chapter titles in a book like this. [Stevie's] Dramatic career, terrible mistakes, stormy love affair, strange situation, and punctured romance. Tinseltown, like Village Studios, combines life and art. Normand depicted the "pride of Yorktown and the apple of her mother's eye." Nicks felt the same way.

In 1985, at a low point in her life, Nicks "felt the union" with Normand after seeing something about her on television. "Every song on 24 Karat Gold is a lifetime," Nicks stated when the album was released. Each... has a soul, a purpose, and a love story. They depict my life behind the scenes, including secrets, broken hearts, broken-hearted people, and survivors. The album is a collection of memories, including "walking on the edge" and a "dangerous year in my life," as well as "what drugs can do to you." Nicks revealed details about "Mabel Normand" in an interview with Billboard, believing, or wanting to believe, the actor's lethal habits, despite the fact that tuberculosis killed her:

Did listening to songs you wrote years ago evoke memories of a specific period in your life?

Yes. Give "Mabel Normand" more attention. Mabel was a fantastic 1920s actress and comedian who also had a severe cocaine addiction. She died of tuberculosis, but her drug addiction killed her. She was in love with a famous director, who was assassinated while attempting to wean her off cocaine. Rumours suggest that he was murdered by drug dealers. When I was at my lowest point following the blow, I watched a documentary about her. I was watching TV one night when the movie came on, and I immediately connected with her. That is when I came up with the song. I attended Betty Ford Rehabilitation Center less than a year later.

Didn't a doctor warn you in the 1980s that if you smoked another line of coke, you'd have a heart attack?

He actually said I would have a brain haemorrhage. The documentary terrified me because it showed this beautiful girl deteriorating so quickly. Sometimes you can't see it in yourself, but you can definitely see it in others. Suicide was not an option for me. I am a generally cheerful person. I used to be happy. I had become addicted to coke, which was a terrible drug for me. It was clearly a bad drug for Mabel as well. She had a gang of rich kids, just like Lindsay Lohan does now. Every fifteen years, the same group of girls appears.

Nicks expanded on her thoughts for the magazine Out, expressing surprise that stars in their twenties fought against themselves in the same way she had. She also described taking stark, unsmiling, unmediated, and unfeminine photos of herself with a Polaroid camera every night and staring in horror at the effects of addiction. (Some of the images appear in the standard edition of 24 Karat Gold.) Nicks wrote "Mabel Normand" as a form of "just say no" warning. "I wanted it to be something that someone struggling with drugs could sit down and listen to 5,000 times," she told Michael Martin at the time. "Try to let it be an epiphany for you, 18-year-old dope addict smoking heroin and taking ecstasy on a dead-end road to hell." I want anyone who hears a doctor say, 'Would you like me to write you a prescription for Klonopin?' to get up, scream, and run out of the room, deflating that doctor's tires. "I want them to hear the word 'cocaine' and think 'brain haemorrhage, beauty gone, lines, ageing, fat.'"

The lyrics to "Mabel Normand" (the album's longest track) combine references to Normand and Taylor's romance, as well as Taylor's conversation with Nicks about addiction. It's a bitter, hard-edged, and aimless composition, similar in tone to Jon Boorstin's piece on the actor's near-greatness. He believes Normand died too soon to create the magnificent black-and-white sound picture she was capable of. Her death marked the end of the silent era; she only performed screen tests for sound films. Her tragedy was a comedy. Boorstin adds, "She's in the movie business." In some of the photographs, Nicks is an inch taller than Normand. She is in the music industry. The lyrics include additional references to Buckingham Palace. Nicks' songs "Races Are Run" and "Long Distance Winner" are reflected in the winning and losing phrases scattered throughout. In the demo, Nicks recites the long verses over a crude synthesised pulse and three chords (A minor, F, and G major, repeated agitatedly). The reworked version is one half step higher.

Wachtel fills the void with overdriven solo fills and, like on "24 Karat Gold," layers acoustic and electric guitars in a style reminiscent of Jess Lynne's work with Tom Petty and the Travelling Wilburys. The guitar playing reflects a broader trend among "legacy" artists toward more natural and traditional guitar and bass playing. Modulations, reverbs, and delays from the 1980s are no longer used.

The first and last verses are about "Sad Mabel Normand"; the middle verses are about "you and your friend" and a "Beloved Exile." Arthuriana, a 1984 novel by popular fantasy writer Parke Godwin, appears to be the starting point. It is titled Beloved Exile and tells the story of Queen Guinevere following King Arthur's death. She appears at his funeral dressed in a "sodden blanket of weariness," "naked to the moment," according to Godwin's colourful prose.27 Several adaptations of the original Arthurian legend show Guinevere falling in love with Lancelot, Arthur's leading knight, and then fleeing to a convent to repent after the king's death in the Battle of Camlann. Godwin picks up where the legend leaves off, portraying Guinevere in an entirely positive light. The Celtic Briton queen is captured by Saxons and sold as a slave, but she eventually joins the "invaders" after learning of Arthur's violence against them.28 Godwin describes her as kind-hearted, forgiving, and altruistic, as opposed to scheming, treacherous, and immoral.

Lancelot and Arthur are both hotly contested roles in Nicks' and Normand's lives, respectively. What does the song reveal about each of them? People's lives do not provide simple explanations, so don't look for one. The singing is characterised by attack, conviction, and focus. It criticises, condemns, and debates itself; it is impulsive; it has the tired-of-the-sheer-waste-of-it-all edginess of multiple takes that could have been just one; it is free and easy; and it is trapped in a three-chord cycle of denial. "Mabel Normand" is sympathetic and circumspect, as is Godwin's reimagined Guinevere. It's a wild ride with no melody, going nowhere and everywhere before coming to a halt with the delirious, punchy, and ultimately unbearable phrase "so beautiful."

The contents of this book may not be copied, reproduced or transmitted without the express written permission of the author or publisher. Under no circumstances will the publisher or author be responsible or liable for any damages, compensation or monetary loss arising from the information contained in this book, whether directly or indirectly. .

Disclaimer Notice:

Although the author and publisher have made every effort to ensure the accuracy and completeness of the content, they do not, however, make any representations or warranties as to the accuracy, completeness, or reliability of the content. , suitability or availability of the information, products, services or related graphics contained in the book for any purpose. Readers are solely responsible for their use of the information contained in this book

Every effort has been made to make this book possible. If any omission or error has occurred unintentionally, the author and publisher will be happy to acknowledge it in upcoming versions.

Copyright © 2024

All rights reserved.

Printed in Great Britain
by Amazon